Cambridge First Certificate in English 5

Cambridge
First Certificate
in English
5

Examination papers from the
University of Cambridge
Local Examinations Syndicate

CAMBRIDGE
UNIVERSITY PRESS

PUBLISHED BY THE PRESS SYNDICATE OF THE UNIVERSITY OF CAMBRIDGE
The Pitt Building, Trumpington Street, Cambridge, United Kingdom

CAMBRIDGE UNIVERSITY PRESS
The Edinburgh Building, Cambridge CB2 2RU, UK
40 West 20th Street, New York, NY 10011–4211, USA
477 Williamstown Road, Port Melbourne, VIC 3207, Australia
Ruiz de Alarcón 13, 28014 Madrid, Spain
Dock House, The Waterfront, Cape Town 8001, South Africa

http://www.cambridge.org

First published 2001
Third printing 2001

Printed in the United Kingdom at the University Press, Cambridge

ISBN 0 521 799163 Student's Book
ISBN 0 521 799171 Student's Book (with answers)
ISBN 0 521 79918X Teacher's Book
ISBN 0 521 799198 Set of 2 Cassettes

Contents

Thanks and acknowledgements

The publishers are grateful to the following for permission to reproduce copyright material. Whilst every effort has been made to locate the owners of copyright, in some cases this has been unsuccessful. The publishers apologise for any infringement or failure to acknowledge the original sources and will be glad to include any necessary correction in subsequent printings.

The Sunday Times for the extract on p. 29 from 'You had to be there' by Cosmo Landesman; *The Times* for the extract on p. 56 from 'Model pupil' by Jane Laidlaw and the text on p. 68, adapted from 'From first steps to runaway success' by John Goodbody; Summersdale Publishers Ltd for the extract on p. 30 from *Don't Lean Out of the Window: The Inter-Rail Experience* by Stewart Ferris and Paul Bassett, Summersdale Publishers Ltd 1992, new ed. 1999; Tessa Lucas and *Home and Country* for the extract on pp. 32–3 from 'Friendship by post', *Home and Country* 1992; A & C Black for the extract on p. 55 from *So you want to be an actor?* by Adrian Rendle, A & C Black Ltd, 2nd ed. 1991; *Sainsbury's Magazine* for the extract on pp. 58–9 from 'In hot water'; Julia Gregson for the extract on p. 61 from 'Thrills and bills', *Good Housekeeping* magazine, March 1995; *Focus* magazine for the extract on p. 81 from 'Going up the wall', *Focus*, March 1995; Telegraph Group Ltd for the extract on pp. 84–5 from 'No time to Shilly-Chalet', *Weekend Telegraph* 26.2.94, © Telegraph Group Ltd; *BBC Music* magazine for the extract on p. 87 from 'Conduct becoming' by Anne Inglis, *BBC Music* 1994, and the text on p. 98 adapted from 'Footnote' by Charles Osborne, *BBC Music*, Nov. 1993; IPC Magazines for the extract on p. 35 from 'Coining it in the countryside' by Vanessa Berridge, *Woman & Home*; *Marks & Spencer Magazine* for the text on p. 46, adapted from 'Barbara Taylor Bradford', *Marks & Spencer Magazine*, Autumn/Winter 1989; *Empire* magazine for the listening passage in Test 3, Paper 4, Part 4, which was adapted from *Empire* magazine, Aug. 1995, p. 48; *School Leaver* magazine for the listening passage in Test 1, Paper 4, Part 4, adapted from 'Making a break: Working adventures abroad' by BUNAC, published in *School Leaver* magazine, Independent Educational Publishing. The extract on p. 94 is adapted from *The Blue Peter Green Book* by Lewis Bronze, Nick Heathcote and Peter Brown with permission of BBC Worldwide Limited. Copyright © Lewis Bronze, Nick Heathcote and Peter Brown. The text on p. 42 is adapted from 'Downhill Racer' by David Allsop, *Midweek*, Feb. 2–6, 1995. The extract on p. 9 is from MORE POWER TO YOU by Connie Brown Glaser and Barbara Steinberg Smalley. Copyright © 1992 by Connie Brown Glaser and Barbara Steinberg Smalley. By permission of Warner Books. Reprinted with permission from the August 1993 Reader's Digest.

For permission to reproduce copyright photographs:

Ace Photo Agency/Mugshots for p. C2 (bottom); Eye Ubiquitous/Frank Leather for p. C10 (top); Gettyone Stone/Doug Armand for p. C9 (top), /Stewart Cohen for p. C1 (top), /Peter Dokus for p. C3 (top), /Frank Herholdt for p. C8 (bottom); Image Bank/Gabriel M. Covian for p. C10 (bottom), /John P. Kelly for p. C8 (top); Life File/Jeremy Hoare for p. C1 (bottom), C11 (bottom right), /Cliff Threadgold for p. C7 (top); The National Trust for p. 3; Network Photographers for p. C7 (bottom); Photofusion/Peter Olive for p. C2 (top), /Ray Roberts for p. C4 (top); Pictor for p. C11 (bottom centre); Powerstock Zefa for p. C11 (top right), C11 (centre left), /Brad Walker for p. C9 (bottom); Quadrant Picture Library/Simon Everett for p. C11 (top left), /Mike Nicholson 1995 for p. C4 (bottom); The Stock Market for p. C3 (bottom), /Tom Ives 97 for p. C11 (bottom left).

Taken on commission for CUP by: Trevor Clifford for p. C6.

Artwork: Oxford Designers & Illustrators

Picture research by Hilary Fletcher

Design concept by Peter Ducker

Cover design by Dunne & Scully

The cassettes which accompany this book were recorded at Studio AVP, London.

To the student

This book is for candidates preparing for the University of Cambridge Local Examinations Syndicate (UCLES) First Certificate in English Examination (FCE). The FCE examination is widely recognised in commerce and industry and in individual university faculties and other educational institutions.

The collection of four complete practice tests comprises past papers from the Cambridge First Certificate in English Examination set in 1998; you can practise these tests on your own or with the help of your teacher.

The FCE examination is part of a group of examinations developed by UCLES called the Cambridge Main Suite. The Main Suite consists of five examinations that have similar characteristics but are designed for different levels of English language ability. Within the five levels, FCE is at Cambridge Level 3.

Cambridge Level 5 Certificate of Proficiency in English (CPE)
Cambridge Level 4 Certificate in Advanced English (CAE)
Cambridge Level 3 First Certificate in English (FCE)
Cambridge Level 2 Preliminary English Test (PET)
Cambridge Level 1 Key English Test (KET)

The FCE examination consists of five papers:

Paper 1	**Reading**	1 hour 15 minutes
Paper 2	**Writing**	1 hour 30 minutes
Paper 3	**Use of English**	1 hour 15 minutes
Paper 4	**Listening**	40 minutes (approximately)
Paper 5	**Speaking**	14 minutes

Paper 1 Reading
This paper consists of **four parts**. Each part contains a text and some questions. Part 4 may contain two or more shorter related texts. There are **35 questions** in total, including multiple choice, gapped text and matching questions.

Paper 2   Writing

This paper consists of **two parts**. For both parts you have to write between 120 and 180 words. Part 1 is **compulsory**. It provides texts which are sometimes accompanied by visual material to help you write a letter.

In Part 2, there are four tasks from which you **choose one** to write about. The range of tasks from which questions may be drawn includes an article, a report, a composition, a short story and a letter. The last question is based on the set books. These books remain on the list for about two years and you should contact UCLES or the UCLES local secretary in your area, if you wish to have the up-to-date list of set books. If you decide to do the question on the set books, there will be two options from which you can choose **one** to write about.

Paper 3   Use of English

This paper consists of **five parts** and tests your control of English grammar, vocabulary and spelling. There are **65 questions** in total. The tasks include gapfilling exercises, sentence transformation, word formation and error correction.

Paper 4   Listening

This paper contains **four parts**. Each part contains a recorded text or texts and some questions including multiple choice, note-taking, sentence completion and matching. You hear each text twice. There is a total of **30 questions**.

Paper 5   Speaking

This paper consists of **four parts**. The standard test format is two candidates and two examiners. One examiner takes part in the conversation, the other examiner listens and gives marks. You will be given photographs and other visual material to look at and talk about. Sometimes you will talk with the other candidate, sometimes with the examiner and sometimes with both.

Marks and results

The total of marks in each paper is adjusted to 40 marks, so the five papers total 200 marks. Your overall FCE grade is based on the total score gained in all five papers. It is not necessary to achieve a satisfactory level in all five papers in order to pass the examination. Certificates are given to candidates who pass the examination with grade A, B or C. A is the highest. The minimum successful performance in order to achieve a grade C corresponds to about 60% of the total marks. D and E are failing grades. Your Statement of Results will include a graphical profile of your performance in each paper and show your relative performance in each one.

To the student

Further information

For more information about FCE or any other UCLES examination write to:

UCLES EFL
1 Hills Road
Cambridge
CB1 2EU
England

Telephone: +44 1223 553997
Fax: +44 1223 460278
e-mail: efl@ucles.org.uk
www.cambridge-efl.org.uk

Test 1

PAPER 1   READING (1 hour 15 minutes)

Part 1

You are going to read an extract from an article about a National Trust Warden.
Choose from the list **A-I** the most suitable heading for each part (**1-7**) of the extract.
There is one extra heading which you do not need to use. There is an example at the
beginning (**0**).

Mark your answers **on the separate answer sheet**.

A	A minor annoyance
B	What makes him good at the job?
C	Towards agreement
D	The problems of an outdoor life
E	There to stay
F	Getting things done
G	Changes to the environment
H	The most suitable candidate
I	The right qualities for the job

Looking after the countryside   ❧ THE NATIONAL TRUST

The National Trust is an organisation whose aim is to conserve the British countryside. Gill Page visits the Lleyn Peninsula in North Wales and talks to one of the wardens employed by the Trust to look after the beautiful areas it owns.

0 | **I**

Common sense. That's what a National Trust Warden needs, according to Gareth Roberts. 'And you definitely need to be good at handling people, because you're continually dealing with farmers, visitors, conservationists and building firms.'

1

Gareth was born and bred on the Lleyn Peninsula and worked on his parents' farm until he married. About 80 people applied for the post as National Trust Warden for the Lleyn Peninsula. In the end, Gareth's local knowledge and farming experience won him the job, despite his lack of formal training.

2

'I find it particularly helpful that I still farm with my parents and that I can deal with farmers on the same level and be aware of their problems. Also, they can't take me in about anything!' he says. His farming life also means he is well able to cope with the physical demands of the job – erecting fences, planting trees, building walls.

3

Since he has been with the Trust, Gareth says he has come to understand more about nature conservation. 'When I was a youngster,' he recalls, 'I used to pick and press flowers, collect butterfly larvae and old birds' nests. And I thought to myself recently, where would I find all those flowers, the birds' nests, the grasshoppers now? It's really become clear to me that farming has affected the countryside. It's not the farmers' fault – they were just doing what the government told them.'

4

Gareth says that, when he started his job, farmers and conservationists were set against each other. Both sides wanted things done their way. Now they are talking and can see each other's point of view. 'We're at the crossroads and there's just a small step needed to join them together,' says Gareth.

5

Conservation is one of the main aspects of Gareth's work, along with public entry to the Trust's land, tree planting and maintenance, and meeting the Trust's tenant farmers. 'My role is to make sure jobs get finished, with as little fuss and as economically as possible. What I enjoy most is seeing projects completed, although about half my time is spent on reports, signing bills and so on.'

6

Gareth is certainly keen on his job and despite never being off duty, he obviously enjoys every minute of his work, especially talking to the public. Most of them, anyway. 'It's the attitude of some people I dislike,' he admits. 'They just walk into the area, demand everything, then walk out again as if it's their absolute right. Having to be nice to those people gets on my nerves!'

7

But as Gareth says, it's all down to common sense really. So if you've got plenty of that, and you like the idea of an outdoor job, you might think of applying to become a warden like Gareth – but don't expect a job to be available on the Lleyn Peninsula for a good many years!

Part 2

You are going to read a newspaper article about ancient rock art. For questions **8-15** choose the answer (**A**, **B**, **C** or **D**) which you think fits best according to the text.

Mark your answers **on the separate answer sheet**.

Careless tourists scar ancient alpine rock art

Tens of thousands of ancient pictures carved into the rocks at one of France's most important tourist sites are being gradually destroyed. Scientists and researchers fear that the 36,000 drawings on rocks in Mont Bego in the French Alps are being damaged so rapidly that they will not survive for future generations.

The mountain, believed to have once been a site for prayer and worship, is scattered with 4,000-year-old drawings cut into bare rock. They include pictures of cows with horns, cultivated fields and various gods and goddesses. But as the popularity of the site increases, the pictures are being ruined by thoughtless graffiti.

Jean Clottes is the chairman of the International Committee on Rock Art. He says, 'People think that because the pictures have been there so long they will always continue to be there. But if the damage continues at this rate there will be nothing left in 50 years.'

He describes seeing tourists stamping on the drawings, wearing away the rock and definition of the artwork as they do so. Some visitors, he says, even chop off parts to take home as souvenirs.

'When people think they can't take a good enough photograph, they rub the drawings to get a clearer picture,' he said. 'The drawings are polished by the weather, and if the sun is shining and the visitors can't see them properly they simply rub and scrape them to make them look fresher.'

Other researchers describe how people arrive carrying long sticks with sharp ends to scratch their own drawings, or even their names, in the rocks.

But experts are divided over the best way to preserve the drawings. Henry de Lumley, director of the Museum of Natural History in Paris, believes that the only way to save the site is to turn the whole mountain into a 'no-go' area, preventing the public from going there except on guided tours. Otherwise, he says, not only will the site be completely destroyed but important research work will be reduced.

Clottes disagrees. 'The measure proposed by Henry de Lumley is the most severe, and while it is the most effective, it is also certain to bring about protests from people who live there,' he said. 'The site was classified as a historic monument years ago by the Ministry of Culture, and we must do as much as possible to save what is there.'

David Lavergne, the regional architect, also wants to avoid closing the site. 'Henry de Lumley's idea isn't ideal,' he said. 'Our department feels that the best solution is to let people look at the site, but because the area is very big it is difficult to prevent visitors from damaging it. I would prefer that everyone was able to look at it, but the main problem is financial. We do not have the funds to employ the necessary number of guards. We may have to consider charging a fee. There seems to be no prospect of government funding.'

In Nice, Annie Echassoux, who also worked on researching the site, is alarmed that as the mountain becomes easier to reach – tourists can now avoid the three-and-a-half-hour walk by hiring vehicles – the damage will increase rapidly. She thinks that the only solution is to rope off the area and provide guides. 'You can't say the plan can't go ahead because there is no money,' she said. 'That is not good enough. Money must be provided because the Ministry of Culture has classified this area as a historic site. If we don't take steps, we will be responsible for losing the drawings for the next generation.'

8   What does 'they' refer to in line 6?
    A   the rocks
    B   the French Alps
    C   the drawings
    D   the tourist sites

9   Jean Clottes says that people who visit the mountain
    A   do not believe the drawings are old.
    B   believe they are allowed to paint there.
    C   think the drawings should be left alone.
    D   assume the drawings will not change.

10   According to Clottes, some of the visitors to the area have
    A   helped to clean the drawings.
    B   taken bits of the rock home.
    C   been unable to take photographs.
    D   misunderstood what the pictures mean.

11   Henry de Lumley is keen to
    A   set up research projects.
    B   safeguard public rights.
    C   keep out individual visitors.
    D   ban traffic in the area.

12   Clottes disagrees with Henry de Lumley's suggestion because he thinks
    A   it won't work.
    B   visitors will protest about it.
    C   he has a better idea.
    D   it will annoy local people.

13   David Lavergne would prefer to
    A   limit the number of visitors to the site.
    B   arrange security to protect the site.
    C   reduce the overall area of the site.
    D   use tourist fees to finance repairs on the site.

14   Which word best describes Annie Echassoux's attitude?
    A   determined
    B   despairing
    C   unforgiving
    D   understanding

15   This article has been written about Mont Bego to
    A   advertise the closure of the site.
    B   warn visitors about the dangers of the site.
    C   encourage scientists to visit the site.
    D   describe fears about the future of the site.

Part 3

You are going to read a magazine interview with a sportswoman. Eight sentences have been removed from the article. Choose from the sentences **A-I** the one which fits each gap (**16-22**). There is one extra sentence which you do not need to use. There is an example at the beginning (**0**).

Mark your answers **on the separate answer sheet**.

The Netball Captain

In our series on women in sport, Suzie Ellis went to meet England's netball captain.

Kendra Slawinski is captain of England's netball team. When I met her, she'd had a typical day for the weeks leading up to next month's World Championships: a day's teaching at a local school followed by a training session in the local supermarket car park. 'Don't you get strange looks?' I asked her. ' 0 I I might notice cars slow down out of the corner of my eye, but that's all.'

'My whole life now is all about making sure I'm at my absolute best for the Championships,' says Kendra.

' 16 ' These are her fourth World Championships and they are guaranteed to be the biggest ever, with 27 nations taking part.

'We'll have home support behind us, which is so special,' she says. 'And it's important that the reputation of netball in this country should be improved. 17 A home crowd will have expectations and give more support. People will expect us to start the tournament with a good game.'

Their first game is against Barbados and it comes immediately after the opening ceremony. ' 18 They have lots of ability.'

The England team are currently ranked fourth in the world. But, as Kendra points out, the World Championships will be tough. 'You have to push yourself to play each day, there's no rest between games as in a series. And you can still win an international series if you lose the first game. **19** '

In the fifteen years since she has been playing at top level, the sport has become harder, faster. On court, players are more aggressive. 'You don't do all that training not to come out a winner,' says Kendra. ' **20** We're all friendlier after the game.'

Netball is also taking a far more scientific approach to fitness testing.

'It is essential that we all think and train like world-class players,' says Kendra. ' **21** I see my role as supporting and encouraging the rest of the team.'

'From the very beginning, my netball career has always been carefully planned,' she says. ' **22** ' Doubtless she will coach young players in the future, but at the moment her eyes are firmly set on her last big event. As she leads out her team in the opening candlelight ceremony, she is more than likely to have a tear in her eye.

A   But the Championships are different because there's only one chance and you have to be ready to make the most of it.

B   In fact, some of them help me with my speed and ball-skills training.

C   But once the final whistle blows, you become a different person.

D   So I took the decision some time ago that this competition would be the end of it as far as playing is concerned.

E   I'm on a strict timetable to gain maximum fitness for them.

F   As far as I'm aware, we have always beaten them, but they'll be exciting to play.

G   As captain, I think it's important that I have a strong mental attitude and lead by example.

H   As a result of playing here, there will be more pressure than we're used to.

I   I'm too involved in what I'm doing – concentrating on my movements and my feet – to see anything else.

Part 4

You are going to read a magazine article about job interviews. For questions **23-35**, decide which of the people hold these opinions. Choose from the list of people (**A-I**). Some of the people may be chosen more than once. When more than one answer is required, these may be given in any order. There is an example at the beginning (**0**).

Mark your answers **on the separate answer sheet**.

People			
A	Mary Pearce	**F**	Albert Mehrabian
B	Head Teacher	**G**	Sheila Rice
C	Simon Grant	**H**	David Artesio
D	Janet Goodwood	**I**	Marian Woodall
E	Director of Personnel		

Which person or people hold(s) these opinions?

You should not talk too much.

0	I

You should not appear too keen.

23	

Interviewees should prepare what they want to say.

24		25	

The more important the job, the better you should dress.

26	

Interviewers can tell how candidates feel.

27		28	

Punctuality is more important than appearance.

29	

Faulty communication can affect your chances of success.

30		31	

The way you dress reflects your attitude to a job.

32		33	

Character is not the interviewer's main interest.

34	

People should be able to wear what they like.

35	

INTERVIEW TIPS

First impressions are often lasting ones. Studies show that people form impressions about us within the first few minutes of meeting. They observe how we dress, our eye contact, our body movement and how fast or slowly we talk, our volume and tone of voice as well as our actual words.

Mary Pearce studied to be a teacher. She says, 'I worked hard to earn my degree. When I finally graduated I was very confident.' She applied for a job at a nearby primary school and got an interview with the Head Teacher. 'I noticed a small hole in my jacket that morning,' she recalls. 'I would have changed, but I knew it would make me late, and I always think it's important to be on time.' Mary didn't get the job. In fact, one of her friends who also teaches at the school told her the **Head Teacher's** only comment was, 'If someone doesn't take the time to present her best image at an interview, what kind of teacher is she going to be?'

As **Simon Grant**, hotel manager, says: 'Interviewees who look as if they care about themselves are more likely to care about their jobs. People think it's what's inside that counts, but in an interview you should aim to come across in the best possible way.'

Yet many people ignore the importance of having a professional image. For example, **Janet Goodwood** worked for ten years as an administrative assistant in a large accounting firm. When the office manager retired, she applied for the position but wasn't even given an interview. 'I thought it was a mistake so I asked the **Director of Personnel** what had happened,' she says. 'He told me I didn't fit the image of an office manager. He suggested I improve my wardrobe before I applied again for promotion. I was shocked. I do a very good job and the way I dress shouldn't make any difference.'

Movement and gestures will also influence an interviewer's first impression of a candidate. Psychologist **Albert Mehrabian** has discovered that 7% of any message about our feelings and attitudes comes from the words we use, 38% from our voice and a surprising 55% from our facial expressions. When our facial expressions and our words send different messages the listener will put more weight on the non-verbal message. So make sure your words agree with your body language. Mixed messages will only confuse the interviewer.

It is also important not to appear too desperate for the job or too eager to please. When **Sheila Rice,** a marketing specialist, applied for a promotion her interview went so well she was offered the job on the spot. 'I was delighted,' she recalls. 'But I reacted to the offer with too much enthusiasm. Once the boss sensed how excited I was, he knew I wasn't going to turn him down. Consequently, he offered me a lower salary than I'd hoped for. I'm sure I could have got more had I managed to control my excitement.'

Finally, a consideration of what we say and how we say it will contribute to the success of an interview. **David Artesio**, the manager of an employment agency, suggests that it's a good idea to inform yourself about the company before you go for an interview. 'The annual report, for example, will tell you about areas of company involvement. Mention an area that interests you during the interview. This will give a positive note and convince others of your interest in the company.'

Business consultant **Marian Woodall** suggests you have a few questions ready and avoid speaking in long, confused sentences. As she puts it, 'Poor communicators talk in paragraphs. Successful communicators talk in short sentences and even in highlighted points.'

PAPER 2 WRITING (1 hour 30 minutes)

Part 1

You **must** answer this question.

1   You are staying in Britain and have recently been to a local art exhibition. You enjoyed the exhibition but you have some suggestions to make so that the next one will be better organised.

Read the advertisement for the exhibition and the notes you have made beside it. Then write a letter to the organiser, giving your opinion of this year's exhibition and making your suggestions for next year.

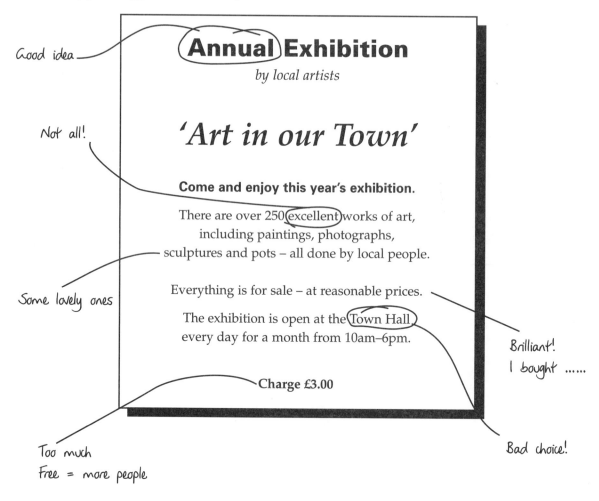

Good idea

Not all!

Some lovely ones

Too much
Free = more people

Annual Exhibition
by local artists

'Art in our Town'

Come and enjoy this year's exhibition.

There are over 250 excellent works of art, including paintings, photographs, sculptures and pots – all done by local people.

Everything is for sale – at reasonable prices.

The exhibition is open at the Town Hall every day for a month from 10am–6pm.

Charge £3.00

Brilliant!
I bought ......

Bad choice!

Write a **letter** of between **120** and **180** words in an appropriate style on the opposite page. Do not write any addresses.

Question 1

Part 2

Write an answer to **one** of the questions 2-5 in this part. Write your answer in **120-180** words in an appropriate style on the next page. Put the question number in the box.

2 You work as a local tour guide. An international travel company has asked you to write a report on a new hotel which has just opened in your town. You should comment in the report on the hotel's facilities **and** say whether you think the hotel would be suitable for international tourists.

   Write your **report**.

3 You have been invited to write a short story for an international young people's magazine. The story must **begin** with the words:

   When they met for the first time, Paul knew immediately that they would be good friends.

   Write your **story**.

4 This is part of a letter which you received from a pen friend:

   > *My neighbours are visiting your country this year for their first ever holiday abroad and they want to know about the food and drink. What typical dishes would you recommend? What do people usually have to drink?*

   Write a **letter**, giving your pen friend the relevant information. Do not write any addresses.

5 Answer **one** of the following two questions based on your reading of one of these set books. Write (**a**) or (**b**) as well as the number **5** in the question box, and the **title** of the book next to the box.
   Great Expectations – Charles Dickens
   Crime Never Pays – Oxford Bookworms Collection
   Rebecca – Daphne du Maurier
   The Old Man and the Sea – Ernest Hemingway
   Tales of Mystery and Imagination – Edgar Allan Poe

   Either (a) Which character in the book or in one of the short stories do you most dislike? Write a **composition**, giving the reasons for your choice.

   Or (b) *TALKING BOOKS* – recordings of well-known books on cassettes – are becoming very popular. You have been asked to write an **article** for an English magazine, saying how well the book or one of the short stories you have read would work on cassette, and what some of the problems might be.

Question

PAPER 3   USE OF ENGLISH (1 hour 15 minutes)

Part 1

For questions **1-15**, read the text below and decide which answer (**A**, **B**, **C** or **D**) best fits each space. There is an example at the beginning (**0**).

Mark your answers **on the separate answer sheet**.

Example:

0   **A**   causes   **B**   results   **C**   leads   **D**   invents

```
0 | A   B   C   D
    -   =   =   =
```

TRAFFIC IN OUR CITIES

The volume of traffic in many cities in the world today continues to expand. This
(0) ..... many problems, including serious air pollution, lengthy delays, and the greater
risk **(1)** ..... accidents. Clearly, something must be done, but it is often difficult to
(2) ..... people to change their habits and leave their cars at home.

One possible **(3)** ..... is to make it more expensive for people to use their cars by
(4) ..... charges for parking and **(5)** ..... tougher fines for anyone who **(6)** ..... the
law. In addition, drivers could be required to pay for using particular routes at different
times of the day. This system, **(7)** ..... as 'road pricing', is already being introduced in a
(8) ..... of cities, using a special electronic card **(9)** ..... to the windscreen of the car.

Another way of **(10)** ..... with the problem is to provide cheap parking on the
(11) ..... of the city, and strictly control the number of vehicles allowed into the centre.
Drivers and their passengers then use a special bus service for the **(12)** ..... stage of
their journey.

Of course, the most important **(13)** ..... is to provide good public transport. However,
to get people to **(14)** ..... the comfort of their cars, public transport must be felt to be
reliable, convenient and comfortable, with fares **(15)** ..... at an acceptable level.

1 **A** of   **B** for   **C** about   **D** by

2 **A** make   **B** arrange   **C** suggest   **D** persuade

3 **A** approach   **B** manner   **C** custom   **D** style

4 **A** enlarging   **B** increasing   **C** growing   **D** developing

5 **A** carrying down **B** putting off **C** bringing in **D** taking away

6 **A** crosses   **B** refuses   **C** breaks   **D** cracks

7 **A** named   **B** seen   **C** called   **D** known

8 **A** quantity   **B** number   **C** total   **D** sum

9 **A** fixed   **B** joined   **C** built   **D** placed

10 **A** doing   **B** handling   **C** dealing   **D** solving

11 **A** outskirts   **B** border   **C** outside   **D** limit

12 **A** late   **B** end   **C** complete   **D** final

13 **A** thought   **B** thing   **C** work   **D** event

14 **A** pass on   **B** throw away   **C** give up   **D** leave out

15 **A** taken   **B** kept   **C** given   **D** stood

8+5+6+10+6 = 35 /65

Part 2

For questions **16-30**, read the text below and think of the word which best fits each space. Use only **one** word in each space. There is an example at the beginning (**0**). Write your answers **on the separate answer sheet**.

Example: | **0** | *more* |

UNIDENTIFIED FLYING OBJECTS

Franklin Roberts was a commercial airline pilot with **(0)** ..*more*.. than 21,000 hours of flying time behind him. However, in **(16)** .... of his great experience, he could not explain something **(17)** .... happened to him in the summer of 1981. As he was flying over Lake Michigan, an object appeared in the sky which took him completely **(18)** .... surprise. Whatever it was, it raced through the sky ahead **(19)** .... his plane and then turned across his path, before finally disappearing **(20)** .... the distance.

(21) .... is the kind of incident that fascinates Richard Haines, a psychologist **(22)** .... works at a research institute in California, and investigates reports like these **(23)** .... a hobby. Over the last twelve years, he **(24)** .... collected thousands of reports on UFOs seen by plane crews. He has concentrated **(25)** .... the stories told to him by pilots, **(26)** .... he believes they are more likely to be accurate. Pilots are trained in observation and make reliable witnesses. They would generally know what they were looking at **(27)** .... it were something familiar. Critics of Haines's work say that there is, in fact, **(28)** .... special about pilots. They claim that pilots are as capable of making mistakes as **(29)** .... else. However, none of this has stopped Haines, who continues to investigate UFO reports **(30)** .... enthusiasm.

Part 3

For questions **31-40**, complete the second sentence so that it has a similar meaning to the first sentence, using the word given. **Do not change the word given**. You must use between **two** and **five** words, including the word given.

Here is an example (**0**).

Example:

0   You must do exactly what the manager tells you.

   carry

   You must ………………………………… instructions exactly.

   The gap can be filled by the words 'carry out the manager's' so you write:

0	carry out the manager's

Write **only** the missing words **on the separate answer sheet**.

---

31   'If I were you Jane, I'd take an umbrella and a raincoat!' said Annabel.

   advised

   Annabel …ADVISED JANE TO TAKE… an umbrella and a raincoat. ¹/₂

32   Nobody apart from my mother thought I would win the race.

   person

   My mother …WAS THE ONLY PERSON WHO… thought I would win the race. ✔

33   Thomas would have gone to the meeting if he had not been so tired.

   tired

   Thomas was …TOO TIRED TO GO… to the meeting. ✔

34   The switchboard operator connected me to the manager.

   put

   The switchboard operator ……PUT MY CALL THROUGH TO…… the manager.

35 There are very few buildings in the old city higher than this.

one

This is ..ONE.....OF..THE..HIGHEST........ buildings in the old city. ⟵

36 If we'd arrived a moment later we would have missed the ferry.

in

We arrived ..JUST..IN..TIME..TO..CATCH........ the ferry.
GET

37 Andrew set off for the supermarket despite the heavy rain.

though

Andrew set off for the supermarket, even THOUGH IT WAS RAINING THE RAIN IS........ heavily.

38 He decided that it wasn't worth continuing the course.

point

He decided that ..THERE IS.....NOT LITTLE POINT......... continuing the course.

39 The cinema was practically empty.

hardly

ANYBODY
ANY PEOPLE
There .IS..HARDLY....FULL IN IN........ the cinema.
WAS

40 We couldn't solve the problem.

solution

We were unable ..TO..FIND..THE..SOLUTION..TO.. the problem.

6

Part 4

For questions **41-55**, read the text below and look carefully at each line. Some of the lines are correct, and some have a word which should not be there.

If a line is correct, put a tick (✓) by the number **on the separate answer sheet**. If a line has a word which should **not** be there, write the word **on the separate answer sheet**. There are two examples at the beginning (**0** and **00**).

Examples:

0	✓
00	to

LETTER OF APPLICATION

0	As you will see from my curriculum vitae, I have
00	attended to university, where I studied English and
41	Law. After finishing my course, I took out a job in a ✗ OUT
42	travel agency in Paris and now I organise few tours ✓ FEW
43	for people who wanting to go to Australia and the United ✗ WHO ✓
44	States. Although I enjoy this very much, I feel I need to get ✓
45	more experience and it would seems to me that working as ✗ WOULD ✓
46	a specialised tour guide in England would help me for do ✗ FOR ✓
47	that. I would rather work in an English-speaking ✓
48	country, as I need to practise my English. I spent one ✓
49	year at London University, which it was most useful. I ✗ IT ✓
50	did much conversation classes and at first I thought that ✗ MUCH ✓
51	I would find them difficult. However, they turned out ✓
52	to be very enjoyable. I will have no any difficulty in ✗ NO ANY
53	coming to England for an interview if you will let me know ✗ WILL ✓
54	in plenty of the time. I enclose details of my present ✗ THE ✓
55	employer who will be too pleased to send you a reference. ✗ TOO

NO

Part 5

For questions **56-65**, read the text below. Use the word given in capitals at the end of each line to form a word that fits in the space in the same line. There is an example at the beginning (**0**). Write your answers **on the separate answer sheet**.

Example: | **0** | *discoveries* |

BOOKS

Nearly all the (**0**) *discoveries*. that have been made through the ages	**DISCOVER**
can be found in books. The (**56**) ..... of the book is one of humankind's	**INVENT**
greatest (**57**) ..... , the importance of which cannot be overestimated.	**ACHIEVE**
Books are very adaptable, providing us with both (**58**) ..... and information.	**ENTERTAIN**
The (**59**) ..... of books began in Ancient Egypt, though not in a form that	**PRODUCE**
is (**60**) ..... to us today. The books read by the Romans, however, have	**RECOGNISE**
some (**61**) ..... to the ones we read now. Until the middle of the 15th	**SIMILAR**
century, in Europe, all books were (**62**) ..... by hand. They were often	**WRITE**
beautifully illustrated and always rare and (**63**) ..... . With printing came	**EXPENSE**
the (**64**) ..... of cheap, large-scale publication and distribution of books,	**POSSIBLE**
making (**65**) ..... more widespread and accessible.	**KNOW**

08-04-04

PAPER 4   LISTENING (approximately 40 minutes)

Part 1

You will hear people talking in eight different situations. For questions **1-8**, choose the best answer, **A**, **B** or **C**.

1   You hear a woman talking to a railway official.
    What is the situation?

   A   She refuses to pay extra.

   B   She hasn't got a ticket.

   C   She wants to leave her luggage.

	1

2   You hear someone being interviewed on the radio.
    Who is the speaker?

   A   a tourist guide

   B   a teacher

   C   a writer

	2

3   Listen to this woman talking on the telephone to a shop assistant
    about something she has bought.
    What feeling does she express?

   A   amusement

   B   disbelief

   C   shock

	3

4   Listen to this student talking to her friend.
    What does she want him to do?

   A   hand in her homework

   B   do her homework

   C   collect her homework

	4

5 Listen to this man reporting on the radio about a football match.
What was the result of the match?

A Liverpool won.

B Newcastle won.

C It was a draw.

	5

6 You overhear two people talking about a film.
What does the woman think about it?

A It is realistic.

B It is inaccurate.

C It has some exciting parts.

	6

7 In a hotel, you overhear a woman talking to a group of people.
Who are they?

A tourists

B staff members

C journalists

	7

8 Listen to this woman inviting a friend to go on holiday.
Where are they going to stay?

A in a tent

B in a hotel

C in a caravan

	8

Part 2

You will hear part of a radio programme about a competition students can enter in order to win a visit to the European Space Agency. For questions **9-18**, fill in the answers.

When does the competition take place? **9**

How many winners will there be? **10**

What is the environment in the plane compared to? **11**

How long will the passengers feel weightless? **12**

Who chooses the winners of the competition? **13**

How many previous competitions have there been? **14**

What did the students put in the table to stop the pizza moving? **15**

What happened to the pizza slices after they had been cut? **16**

What nationality were the students who did the candle experiment? **17**

What shape was the flame of the candle? **18**

Part 3

You will hear five different people talking about their work, which is in some way connected with crime. For questions **19-23**, choose from the list **A-F** who each speaker is. Use the letters only once. There is one extra letter which you do not need to use.

A   a policeman

Speaker 1 | 19

B   a novel writer

Speaker 2 | 20

C   a lawyer

Speaker 3 | 21

D   a judge

Speaker 4 | 22

E   a doctor

Speaker 5 | 23

F   a reporter

Part 4

You will hear part of a radio programme about an organisation called BUNAC, which helps British students find temporary work in the USA, Canada and Australia. For questions **24-30**, decide which of the statements are TRUE and which are FALSE. Write **T** for **TRUE** or **F** for **FALSE** in the box provided.

24 It is easier to find work abroad with voluntary organisations. | 24 |

25 Only university students can apply to work in a summer camp. | 25 |

26 You can only get a free flight if you work with children. | 26 |

27 You can work in Canada for longer than in the USA. | 27 |

28 Kathryn worked in an office in Australia for a year before travelling around. | 28 |

29 Kathryn's experience has made her feel more sure of herself. | 29 |

30 BUNAC will provide help if you get into difficulties. | 30 |

PAPER 5   SPEAKING (14 minutes)

You take the Speaking test with another candidate, referred to here as your partner. There are two examiners. One will speak to you and your partner and the other will be listening. Both examiners will award marks.

Part 1 (3 minutes)

The examiner asks you and your partner questions about yourselves. You may be asked about things like 'your home town', 'your interests', 'your career plans', etc.

Part 2 (4 minutes)

The examiner gives you two photographs and asks you to talk about them for one minute. The examiner then asks your partner a question about your photographs and your partner responds briefly.

Then the examiner gives your partner two different photographs. Your partner talks about these photographs for one minute. This time the examiner asks you a question about your partner's photographs and you respond briefly.

Part 3 (3 minutes)

The examiner asks you and your partner to talk together. You may be asked to solve a problem or try to come to a decision about something. For example, you might be asked to decide the best way to use some rooms in a language school. The examiner gives you a picture to help you but does not join in the conversation.

Part 4 (4 minutes)

The examiner joins in the conversation. You all talk together in a more general way about what has been said in Part 3. The examiner asks you questions but you and your partner are also expected to develop the conversation.

Test 2

PAPER 1   READING (1 hour 15 minutes)

Part 1

You are going to read a newspaper article about people who go to watch TV programmes being made. Choose from the list **A-I** the sentence which best summarises each part (**1-7**) of the article. There is one extra sentence which you do not need to use. There is an example at the beginning (**0**).

Mark your answers **on the separate answer sheet**.

A	Studio audiences consist of all kinds of people.
B	For some people, being in a studio audience is preferable to watching television at home.
C	Common ideas about what happens when you are in a studio audience are not always correct.
D	Studio audiences play an important part in the making of television programmes.
E	Members of studio audiences are sometimes not regarded with respect.
F	Despite the disadvantages, it is enjoyable to be in a studio audience.
G	It is hard for some people to understand the reasons for wanting to be in a studio audience.
H	People become part of a studio audience for various reasons.
I	Viewers wonder what kind of people are in studio audiences.

Studio Audiences

· ·

What's it like to be in the audience when a television programme is being made? Cosmo Landesman found out.

0	I

Like technical difficulties, studio audiences are just another common feature of television life, and yet to many of us they remain a mystery. Watching them getting excited on game shows, for example, we sit back and ask ourselves – just who are these people?

1	

Of all the audiences for live entertainment, the studio variety is widely considered to be the lowest of the low. I have heard it said that even people who work in television treat studio audiences with scorn – or, as one cameraman put it, 'like cattle'.

2	

I had assumed that studio audiences were made up of silly people desperate for two seconds of fame. But there's no such thing as a typical studio audience. They come from all classes, professions and income groups. Television tries to attract different types of people for different types of programme.

3	

Those of us who prefer to watch television from home can't see why anyone would want to watch television from a studio. Why would anyone bother to apply for tickets, travel long distances, and suffer hours of boredom in the discomfort of a studio just to watch what they can see at home?

4	

One theory is that people hope that for a second they might appear on television. I didn't believe this until I spoke to Angela. Why had she come? 'It was a chance to appear on television.' Another theory is that people are curious to take a look behind the scenes. But the most common explanation I heard was simply a case of 'a friend gave me a ticket'.

5	

Few of us have ever sat in a studio audience, yet we think we can imagine what it is like. You sit there, squashed among strangers, while someone flashes cards with APPLAUD or LAUGH on them – and you clap or laugh accordingly. This may reflect the reality of some television, but not all by any means. As one studio manager puts it, 'We always assume a show will be good enough not to need these signs.'

6	

But is there any real difference between what you experience in a studio and what you see on your television at home? For Claire, sitting in a studio is 'more exciting', while Charlotte liked the feeling of involvement with live television. 'Last year I saw my favourite comedian. When you see him on television at home you miss out on a lot.'

7	

What I missed out on was the sight of live actors – from where I was sitting all I could see was the back of somebody's head. The opening scenes were shot so far from where I sat that I ended up watching the show on a studio monitor. Going to a studio may be a terrible way to watch television, but that's not what's important. For most of the audience it was simply fun and a free night of entertainment.

Part 2

You are going to read an extract from a book. For questions **8-14**, choose the answer
(**A**, **B**, **C** or **D**) which you think fits best according to the text.

Mark your answers **on the separate answer sheet**.

I was dirty, smelly, hungry and somewhere beneath all that, suntanned. It was the end of an
Inter-Rail holiday. My body couldn't take any more punishment. My mind couldn't deal with any
more foreign timetables, currencies or languages.

'Never again,' I said, as I stepped onto home ground. I said exactly the same thing the following
year. And the next. All I had to do was buy one train ticket and, because I was under twenty-five years
old, I could spend a whole month going anywhere I wanted in Europe. Ordinary beds are never the
same once you've learnt to sleep in the corridor of a train, the rhythm rocking you into a deep sleep.

Carrying all your possessions on your back in a rucksack makes you have a very basic approach to
travel, and encourages incredible wastefulness that can lead to burning socks that have become too
10 anti-social, and getting rid of books when finished. On the other hand, this way of looking at life
is entirely in the spirit of Inter-Rail, for common sense and reasoning can be thrown out of the
window along with the paperback book and the socks. All it takes to achieve this carefree attitude is
one of those tickets in your hand.

Any system that enables young people to travel through countries at a rate of more than one a day
must be pretty special. On that first trip, my friends and I were at first unaware of the possibilities of
this type of train ticket, thinking it was just an inexpensive way of getting to and from our chosen
camp-site in southern France. But the idea of non-stop travel proved too tempting, for there was always
just one more country over the border, always that little bit further to go. And what did the extra miles
cost us? Nothing.

We were not completely uninterested in culture. But this was a first holiday without parents, as it
was for most other Inter-Railers, and in organising our own timetable we left out everything
except the most immediately available sights. This was the chance to escape the guided tour, an
opportunity to do something different. I took great pride in the fact that, in many places, all I could
be bothered to see was the view from the station. We were just there to get by, and to have a good time
doing so. In this we were no different from most of the other Inter-Railers with whom we shared
corridor floors, food and water, money and music.

The excitement of travel comes from the sudden reality of somewhere that was previously just
a name. It is as if the city in which you arrive never actually existed until the train pulls in at the
29 station and you are able to see it with your own tired eyes for the first time.

Only by actually seeing Europe, by watching the changing landscapes and seeing the differences in
attitudes and lifestyles, can you really have an accurate picture of the continent in your mind.
Everybody knows what is there, but it is meaningless until you view it yourself. This is what makes
other people's holiday photos so boring.

While the train trip won't allow you to discover anything new in the world sense, it is a valuable
personal experience. Europe is a big place, and Inter-Rail gives people the best opportunity to
recognise this ... though in our case it didn't happen immediately.

8 At the end of his first trip, the writer said 'Never again' because

    A he felt ill.

    B he disliked trains.

    C he was tired from the journey.

    D he had lost money.

9 What does the writer mean by 'this way of looking at life' in line 10?

    A worrying about your clothes

    B throwing unwanted things away

    C behaving in an anti-social way

    D looking after your possessions

10 Why did the writer originally buy an Inter-Rail ticket?

    A to go on a tour of Europe

    B to meet other young people

    C to see a lot of famous places

    D to get to one place cheaply

11 What the writer liked about travelling without his parents was that

    A he could see more interesting places.

    B he could spend more time sightseeing.

    C he could stay away from home longer.

    D he could make his own decisions.

12 On his first trip, the writer found that the other young Inter-Railers were

    A unselfish.

    B irresponsible.

    C badly organised.

    D concerned about money.

13 What does 'it' in line 29 refer to?

    A a name

    B the city

    C the train

    D the station

14 According to the writer, other people's holiday photos can be boring if

    A they are badly taken.

    B they are similar to your own.

    C you haven't visited the same place.

    D you could have done better yourself.

Part 3

You are going to read a magazine article about letter writing. Eight sentences have been removed from the article. Choose from the sentences **A-I** the one which fits each gap (**15-21**). There is one extra sentence which you do not need to use. There is an example at the beginning (**0**).

Mark your answers **on the separate answer sheet**.

Drop me a line!

In our fast world of phones, fax machines and computers, the old-fashioned art of letter writing is at risk of disappearing altogether. **0** **I** There is the excitement of its arrival, the pleasure of seeing who it is from and, finally, the enjoyment of the contents.

Letter writing has been part of my life for as long as I can remember. It probably began with the little notes I would write to my mother. My mother, also, always insisted I write my own thank-you letters for Christmas and birthday presents. **15**

When I left home at 18 to train as a doctor in London, I would write once a week, and so would my mother. Occasionally my father would write and it was always a joy to receive his long, amusing letters. **16** Of course,

we also made phone calls but it is the letters I remember most.

There were also letters from my boyfriends. In my youth I seemed to attract people who had to work or study away at some time and I was only able to stay in touch by correspondence. **17** I found that I could often express myself more easily in writing than by talking.

I love the letters that come with birthday or Christmas cards. **18** And it's better still when it's an airmail envelope with beautiful stamps. My overseas letters arrive from Mangala in Sri Lanka, from someone I trained with over 20 years ago, and I have a penfriend in Australia and another in Vancouver.

Then there's the lady who writes to me from France. If we hadn't started talking in a restaurant on the way home from holiday, if my husband hadn't taken her photo and if I hadn't asked her for her address, I would never have been able to write to her. **19** [ ] As it is, we now have a regular correspondence. I can improve my French (she speaks no English); we have stayed at her home twice and she has stayed with us.

My biggest letter-writing success, however, came this summer, when my family and I stayed with my American penfriend in Texas. **20** [ ] Everyone was amazed that a correspondence could last so long. The local press even considered the correspondence worth reporting on the front page.

I am pleased that my children are carrying on the tradition. Like my mother before me, I insist they write their own thank-you letters. My daughter writes me little letters, just as I did to my mother. **21** [ ] I strongly urge readers not to allow letter writing to become another 'lost art'.

A   Most of the letters from home contained just everyday events concerning my parents and their friends.

B   We had been corresponding for 29 years but had never met.

C   It didn't matter how short or untidy they were as long as they were letters.

D   Notes are appreciated, but how much better to have a year's supply of news!

E   Poor handwriting can spoil your enjoyment of a letter.

F   But instead of harming the relationships, letter writing seemed to improve them.

G   She and my son have penfriends of their own in Texas, organised by my penfriend.

H   More important, if she hadn't replied, we would be the poorer for it.

I   Yet, to me, there is something about receiving a letter that cannot be matched by any other form of communication.

Part 4

You are going to read some information about five women who have started businesses from their homes in the countryside. For questions **22-35**, choose from the women (**A-E**). The women may be chosen more than once. When more than one answer is required, these may be given in any order. There is an example at the beginning (**0**).

Mark your answers **on the separate answer sheet**.

Which woman or women ...

has international contacts?	**0** D	
don't employ anyone?	**22**	**23**
were initially short of money?	**24**	**25**
needs to be available outside office hours?	**26**	
has found a separate workplace?	**27**	
has suffered setbacks in her business?	**28**	
have changed their roles in their companies?	**29**	**30**
charge less to be able to compete more easily?	**31**	**32**
depends only on personal recommendation?	**33**	
has had to make an unpleasant decision?	**34**	
produces work mostly for local people?	**35**	

Running a business in the countryside

Five women talk about their experiences setting up a business in the countryside.

A 'My customers are friends,' says **CHRISTINE HOGAN**, who runs a computer-aided design business with a turnover of over £200,000 a year and four full-time employees. 'My husband and I moved out of London to the country when our children were small, and I wanted work I could do at home. I had worked with computers before I was married, so my husband suggested I set up a computer-aided design business. It needed a huge amount of money and things were difficult in the beginning. But I have been very careful, making sure that I told the bank manager if I was likely to overspend. Being in the house is a big saving, and I can carry on working in the evening if I want. It has remained a small business. We hardly ever deliver work – people from the area tend to collect it from us.'

B 'I enjoy being independent,' says **MAGGY SASANOW**, who works from home as a designer of greetings cards. 'I trained in art at university, and wanted to work in a museum. But when I married, we went to live in the countryside, where there wasn't that sort of work. So I decided to set up my own business and I produce a range of 50 greetings cards which I sell to museums. I work in a big room upstairs. The disadvantage of working from home is that there is always something that needs doing – like mowing the lawn. My business comes completely by word of mouth – I don't advertise at all. People send work down from London as I am cheaper than other artists. Working alone, I don't get to exchange ideas with other people any more, but generally there are more advantages than disadvantages.'

C 'It has been hard at times,' says **DELIA TURNER**, whose curtain-making business has seen good times and bad. 'I started my business eight years ago. Then this type of business was expanding, and in two years my turnover went from £24,000 to £80,000. I used to manage six full-time curtain-makers. But I had to sack them because of the decline in the economy, which was painful because it is not easy to find other jobs in this area. I am right back almost to where I started, making the curtains at home myself, with my husband's help, and using women who work from their homes. I have to be prepared to cut my prices when it's necessary and to look at different opportunities.'

D **TESSA STRICKLAND** runs the editorial and production side of her children's book publishing business from her farmhouse. 'I moved to the countryside three years ago for two reasons. The first was financial, because London was so expensive, and the second was because I love the country. I enjoy being able to work when I want to. Eighty per cent of my income comes from deals with Australia, the Far East and North America, so I have to take calls at odd hours. The disadvantage is that it requires discipline to shut the office door. I publish children's books from cultures around the world, working with authors and artists. All my professional experience had been in London, so I used to feel very alone at first.'

E **MEG RIVERS** runs a cakes-by-post business and a shop with a turnover of £250,000 a year and employs six people, some part-time. 'I started ten years ago at home. I am very interested in health, so I started making fruit cakes, using good quality flour and eggs. Then I started getting requests from friends and relatives, and soon I was sending cakes all over the country. Seven years ago I rented a small building and everything is made there – we have a baker and assistant, and a professional cake-icer. I don't cook at all now, as I run the commercial side. My greatest problem has been the financial side of the business, which has been difficult simply because we didn't have an enormous amount of money to set up with.'

© *Woman & Home/IPC Syndication*

PAPER 2   WRITING (1 hour 30 minutes)

Part 1

You **must** answer this question.

1   You went on a three-day ABC Citybreaks holiday to Bramville. Unfortunately you were very disappointed in the holiday and did not enjoy it.

Read the ABC Citybreaks advertisement and the notes you made below about the holiday. Then, using the information, write a letter to ABC Citybreaks, complaining about the holiday and asking for some money back.

ABC CITYBREAKS TO BRAMVILLE

Bramville has so much to offer: the fascinating Cathedral, the Castle, museums and art galleries, a wide range of shopping.

- Comfortable, quiet 3-star hotels, convenient for the shopping area and all the tourist attractions.

- Quick, easy travel by air, train or coach.

You can always rely on ABC Citybreaks!

City
▶ museums & art galleries were only open on one day
▶ shops disappointing

Hotel
▶ 3-star?! poor quality
▶ very noisy
▶ 30 mins. walk to city centre

Journey home
▶ a disaster!

ASK FOR SOME MONEY BACK

Write a **letter** of between **120** and **180** words in an appropriate style on the opposite page. Do not write any addresses.

Question 1

Part 2

Write an answer to **one** of the questions **2-5** in this part. Write your answer in **120-180** words in an appropriate style on the opposite page. Put the question number in the box.

2   You have seen this in
    an international magazine.

> Write and tell us what you think makes a **perfect friendship**. The winning article will be published in our international magazine and the winner will receive a prize of £1000.

Now write your **article** for the magazine.

3   You have had a class discussion about the following statement:

If you don't make music yourself, you can't enjoy other people's music.

Your teacher has now asked you to write a composition, giving your own views on the statement.

Write your **composition**.

4   This is part of a letter you
    receive from a pen friend.

> Guess what? Now my exams are over, I've decided I'm going to improve my fitness and health. The only problem is I don't know how to start. I know you're very fit – what do you suggest?

Write a **letter**, giving advice to your pen friend. Do not write any addresses.

5   Answer **one** of the following two questions based on your reading of one of these set books. Write (**a**) or (**b**) as well as the number **5** in the question box, and the **title** of the book next to the box.
    Great Expectations – Charles Dickens
    Crime Never Pays – Oxford Bookworms Collection
    Rebecca – Daphne du Maurier
    The Old Man and the Sea – Ernest Hemingway
    Tales of Mystery and Imagination – Edgar Allan Poe

   Either (**a**)   If you could make a film of the book or of one of the short stories you have read, which events would you concentrate on? Write a **composition**, describing these events briefly and explaining their importance to the film.

   Or   (**b**)   In most stories, there is at least one place which readers remember well. From the book or short story you have read, choose one place which stays in your memory. Write a **composition**, describing the place and explaining why it is so special.

Question [   ]

....
....
....
....
....
....
....
....
....
....
....
....
....
....
....
....
....
....
....
....
....
....
....
....
....
....
....
....
....
....
....
....
....

PAPER 3   USE OF ENGLISH (1 hour 15 minutes)

Part 1

For questions **1-15**, read the text below and decide which answer (**A**, **B**, **C** or **D**) best fits each space. There is an example at the beginning (**0**).
Mark your answers **on the separate answer sheet**.

Example:

0   **A**   among   **B**   with   **C**   from   **D**   out

0	A	B	C	D
	⎯	⎯	**_**	⎯

AUDIOBOOKS – BOOKS ON CASSETTE

In the modern world, there is a wealth of leisure activities to choose **(0)** ..... .
Entertainment industries **(1)** ..... for your leisure time. You can watch TV, listen to
music, go to an art gallery or concert or, of course, read a book. Sometimes it seems
that reading is **(2)** ..... because, **(3)** ..... you're a fast reader, it can take a **(4)** .....
amount of time to finish a novel, for example. But in the **(5)** ..... world, time is
something that can be in short supply.

Book publishers haven't been **(6)** ..... to realise this and are now selling a product
which needn't **(7)** ..... as much of your time but still tells you an excellent story. The
new product is the audiobook – cassette recordings of shortened novels, often read by
well-known personalities or the authors themselves. Audiobooks are **(8)** ..... new but
people are becoming more aware of them and sales are increasing **(9)** ..... .

One of the attractions of audiobooks is that they're **(10)** ..... listening to the radio, only
better. You can listen to what you want when you want, and you won't ever **(11)** .....
anything. Much of their appeal **(12)** ..... in their flexibility. They **(13)** ..... you to do
other things while you're listening, such as driving or **(14)** ..... the housework. For some
people, audiobooks can be a much more enjoyable way of **(15)** ..... knowledge than
reading.

1 **A** chase   **B** compete   **C** oppose   **D** pursue

2 **A** neglected   **B** declined   **C** lessened   **D** disposed

3 **A** in spite   **B** no matter   **C** regardless of **D** even if

4 **A** plentiful   **B** broad   **C** considerable   **D** lasting

5 **A** current   **B** new   **C** present   **D** modern

6 **A** behind   **B** slow   **C** delayed   **D** overdue

7 **A** take up   **B** fill out   **C** go through   **D** pass by

8 **A** partly   **B** approximately **C** roughly   **D** relatively

9 **A** ever since then **B** all the time **C** up until now **D** from then on

10 **A** as   **B** same   **C** like   **D** both

11 **A** pass   **B** lack   **C** miss   **D** lose

12 **A** stands   **B** belongs   **C** bases   **D** lies

13 **A** grant   **B** allow   **C** spare   **D** afford

14 **A** doing   **B** running   **C** making   **D** cleaning

15 **A** grasping   **B** catching   **C** gaining   **D** raising

Part 2

For questions **16-30**, read the text below and think of the word which best fits each space. Use only **one** word in each space. There is an example at the beginning (**0**). Write your answers **on the separate answer sheet**.

Example: | 0 | *most* |

THE INFERNO SKI RACE

The Inferno is the oldest and (**0**) ..most.. celebrated of all amateur ski races. (**16**) .... is held every year, on a Saturday in the middle of January, above (**17**) .... remote village of Mürren in Switzerland. Anyone can take part, as (**18**) .... as they belong to a ski racing club and pay the race fee.

The Inferno (**19**) .... , strangely enough, a British invention. The story begins with a former tennis racquet salesman called Henry Lunn, who came up (**20**) .... the idea of the package holiday in the early 1900s and began taking groups of British people to the Alps for winter sports. Henry's son, Arnold, grew very fond (**21**) .... Mürren and he founded a ski club there in 1924, which he called the Kandahar. Four years (**22**) .... , seventeen of the club's members took part (**23**) .... the first Inferno race, from the top of the 2,970 metre Schilthorn mountain to Mürren below.

In those early days, they (**24**) .... to climb for six hours from the railway terminus in Mürren (**25**) .... the start of the race. Today, racers can use a cable car which (**26**) .... about twenty minutes. In the first race, the winning time for the fourteen-kilometre race was one hour, twelve minutes. (**27**) .... days it tends to be almost exactly an hour less. Although the skiers are very (**28**) .... faster now, some things haven't changed. The course, (**29**) .... is steep and has sharp bends, remains (**30**) .... of the most demanding and frightening in the world.

Part 3

For questions **31-40**, complete the second sentence so that it has a similar meaning to the first sentence, using the word given. **Do not change the word given**. You must use between **two** and **five** words, including the word given.

Here is an example (**0**).

Example:

0   You must do exactly what the manager tells you.

carry

You must .... instructions exactly.

The gap can be filled by the words 'carry out the manager's' so you write:

0	carry out the manager's

Write **only** the missing words **on the separate answer sheet**.

---

31   I can't believe this is the best room there is!

better

There must .... this one!

32   The notice says you have to sign the forms twice.

must

The notice says the forms .... twice.

33   I'm sorry but I cannot lend you any money.

me

I'm sorry but it .... to lend you any money.

34   The journey will be about nine hours, whichever route you take.

matter

It .... you take, the journey will be about nine hours.

35 The last time I went to Canada was in January 1994.

been

I .... Canada since January 1994.

36 It's a waste of time for you to discuss the problem with Jane.

point

There's .... the problem with Jane.

37 My house is as big as Peter's.

same

Peter's house .... mine.

38 Michael is usually punctual so I'm surprised that he's late.

like

I'm surprised that Michael's not here yet because it's

.... late.

39 The committee discussed what to do.

discussion

The committee .... should be done.

40 Nobody in the group disagreed with the plan except for John.

exception

With .... , everyone in the group agreed with the plan.

Part 4

For questions **41-55**, read the text below and look carefully at each line. Some of the lines are correct, and some have a word which should not be there.

If a line is correct, put a tick (✓) by the number **on the separate answer sheet**. If a line has a word which should **not** be there, write the word **on the separate answer sheet**. There are two examples at the beginning (**0** and **00**).

Examples:

0	*of*
00	✓

CONGRATULATIONS

0	Congratulations on winning of the tennis championship! You must be
00	very pleased, especially since the prize is quite a lot of money.
41	What are you going to spend it on? You could even buy a new car
42	with all that money! You should have be in great shape after all the
43	training you have been doing. It must be so very hard work, practising
44	all those hours for every day, but it is worth it in the end, isn't it?
45	Perhaps you are thinking of going on holiday so that you can have
46	a break from tennis and relax. Can you tell me exactly what is kind of
47	tennis racquet you chose for the competition? If I would get the same,
48	it might help me to improve my game. Anyway, congratulations on
49	your great victory! I'm still studying English every single day and the
50	course has three months to go. I have moved house, as if you can see
51	from my new address. Make sure you reply back to the right address!
52	Your last letter went to my old address, but it wasn't by your fault
53	because I hadn't told anyone which I had moved then. Did you know that
54	I have had a job for the last three weeks? I work in a restaurant four
55	evenings a week. I like it, but I don't arrive to home until one o'clock in the
	morning, which is a bit inconvenient.

Part 5

For questions **56-65**, read the text below. Use the word given in capitals at the end of each line to form a word that fits in the space in the same line. There is an example at the beginning (**0**). Write your answers **on the separate answer sheet**.

Example: | **0** | lonely |

A POPULAR WRITER

Emma Harte, in Barbara Taylor Bradford's novel, was a poor (**0**) .lonely.. girl	**LONE**
who became the (**56**) ..... owner of an international chain of stores. Like	**WEALTH**
the woman she writes about, Ms Bradford is beautiful and (**57**) ..... . She	**AMBITION**
left school at sixteen and became a (**58**) ..... . After twenty-three	**JOURNAL**
years of this work, she made the (**59**) ..... to start writing novels.	**DECIDE**
She is now one of the most (**60**) ..... -paid novelists in the world. Was Emma	**HIGH**
Harte's story based on Ms Bradford's own (**61**) ..... successful life? 'I'm	**INCREDIBLE**
afraid not,' she said with (**62**) ..... . 'My life has been quite different from	**AMUSE**
Emma Harte's. She was (**63**) ..... to be born into a poor family. I came	**LUCK**
from a middle-class home and I'm (**64**) ..... married to a rich American	**HAPPY**
film producer. The only thing I share with my heroine is her (**65**) ..... to	**ABLE**

work hard.'

PAPER 4   LISTENING (approximately 40 minutes)

Part 1

You will hear people talking in eight different situations. For questions **1-8**, choose the best answer, **A**, **B** or **C**.

1   You hear a woman talking about something she saw.
    Who is the speaker?

   A   a shop worker

   B   a customer

   C   a store detective

2   You hear a teacher talking to her colleagues.
    What does she want them to do?

   A   talk to the school's Head

   B   accompany the students

   C   ask parents to help

3   You hear a man talking about a new purchase.
    What has he just bought?

   A   a van

   B   a motorbike

   C   a car

4   You hear part of a radio play.
    Where is the scene taking place?

   A   a hotel

   B   an office

   C   a house

5 Outside a theatre, you overhear two people talking about the play they have just seen. What did the man like about it?

A the acting

B the story

C the stage design

6 You hear part of a radio programme about the media. What is being reviewed?

A a computer program

B a new book

C a video cassette

7 In a college, you hear a man talking to a group. Who is he talking to?

A new students

B students in the middle of a course

C former students

8 At the airport, you overhear a conversation. How does the woman feel?

A tired

B ill

C nervous

Part 2

You will hear part of a radio programme about bags for walkers. For questions **9-18**, complete the sentences.

Rod's shop sells bags and other | CAMPING, | **9** | equipment. ✓

A backpack could spoil your holiday if it doesn't | FIT (YOUR BACK. | **10** | ✗

A 35-litre bag is good for | 4 DAYS TRIPS | **11** | ✓

An upright bag is recommended for people who are going to | CLIMB | **12** | ✓

To protect breakable items choose a bag with a | SOLID / FIRM BOTTOM / LEATHER BASE | **13** | ✗

A bag with | COMPARTMENTS | **14** | ✓ inside will allow you to separate your belongings.

External pockets can be used to carry tools that are | SHARP | **15** | ✗ or dirty.

It is important that shoulder straps are | EASY TO ADJUST | **16** |

A horizontal bar will prevent shoulder straps from | FALLING | **17** |

Padded parts of the bag should have plenty of | AIR HOLE - AIRHOLES, VENTILATION | **18** | ✗ so that sweat can escape.

Part 3

You will hear five journalists giving reasons for their success. For questions **19-23**, choose from the list **A-F** the reason each journalist gives. Use the letters only once. There is one extra letter which you do not need to use.

A   I deal with the main news.

Speaker 1 | B | **19** | ✓

B   I have my own individual style.

Speaker 2 | C | **20** | ✗ D

C   I express new opinions.

Speaker 3 | A | **21** | ✓

D   I check all my information.

Speaker 4 | E | **22** | ✓

E   I express strong feelings.

Speaker 5 | F | **23** | ✓

F   I deal with problems readers may face.

Part 4

You will hear an interview with a man who makes models for films and television.
For questions **24-30**, choose the best answer, **A**, **B** or **C**.

24   Matt got a job doing holiday relief work because he wanted
   A   to do part-time work.
   B   a career in photography.
   C   to work in television.

C | **24** | ✓

25   What did Matt find 'interesting' about the sixties?
   A   the fascination with space travel
   B   the increased number of comic books
   C   the advances in photography

A | **25** | ✓

26   Why were Matt's models used on the news?
   A   They were better than pictures.
   B   Some equipment had been destroyed.
   C   The studio was trying new ideas.

B *A* | **26** | ✗

27   Matt thinks he was successful at getting work in television because
   A   he had good experience.
   B   he knew some of the staff.
   C   he was available at the right time.

C *B* | **27** | ✗

28   Matt worked on *Bright Star* as
   A   part of a team.
   B   the producer.
   C   a design student.

A *b* | **28** | ✗

29   Matt was invited on children's television to
   A   tell stories about his design work.
   B   explain the purpose of space research.
   C   help children make models themselves.

C | **29** | ✓

30   Matt remembers *Heart of Darkness* because
   A   it was his favourite comedy.
   B   his work was recognised.
   C   a film was made of it.

18/30

B | **30** | ✓

PAPER 5   SPEAKING (14 minutes)

You take the Speaking test with another candidate, referred to here as your partner. There are two examiners. One will speak to you and your partner and the other will be listening. Both examiners will award marks.

Part 1 (3 minutes)

The examiner asks you and your partner questions about yourselves. You may be asked about things like 'your home town', 'your interests', 'your career plans', etc.

Part 2 (4 minutes)

The examiner gives you two photographs and asks you to talk about them for one minute. The examiner then asks your partner a question about your photographs and your partner responds briefly.

Then the examiner gives your partner two different photographs. Your partner talks about these photographs for one minute. This time the examiner asks you a question about your partner's photographs and you respond briefly.

Part 3 (3 minutes)

The examiner asks you and your partner to talk together. You may be asked to solve a problem or try to come to a decision about something. For example, you might be asked to decide the best way to use some rooms in a language school. The examiner gives you a picture to help you but does not join in the conversation.

Part 4 (4 minutes)

The examiner joins in the conversation. You all talk together in a more general way about what has been said in Part 3. The examiner asks you questions but you and your partner are also expected to develop the conversation.

Test 3

PAPER 1   READING (1 hour 15 minutes)

Part 1

You are going to read an extract from a book about becoming an actor. Choose from the list **A-I** the sentence which best summarises each part (**1-7**) of the extract. There is one extra sentence which you do not need to use. There is an example at the beginning (**0**).

Mark your answers **on the separate answer sheet**.

A	There is one main reason why every actor likes acting.
B	It is important to have a realistic attitude to being an actor.
C	There are certain qualities which anyone needs to succeed as an actor.
D	Many actors realise after a while that the profession does not suit them.
E	You should not pay too much attention to comments about your decision to become an actor.
F	Successful actors don't claim to understand what it takes to be a successful actor.
G	It is difficult but not impossible to succeed as an actor.
H	Actors learn to deal with the unpleasant aspects of the profession.
I	If you decide to become an actor, your chances of succeeding are not good.

So you want to be an actor

0 | I

If you tell someone that you want to make a career as an actor, you can be sure that within two minutes the word 'risky' will come up. And, of course, acting is a very risky career – let there be no mistake about that. The supply of actors is far greater than the demand for them.

1 | E ✓

Once you choose to become an actor, many people who you thought were your closest friends will tell you you're crazy, though some may react quite differently. No two people will give you the same advice. But it is a very personal choice you are making, and only you can take responsibility for yourself and for realising your ambition.

2 | C G

There are no easy ways of getting there – no written examinations to pass, and no absolute guarantee that when you have successfully completed your training you will automatically make your way in the profession. It's all a matter of luck plus talent. Yet there is a demand for new faces and new talent, and there is always the prospect of excitement, glamour and the occasional rich reward.

3 | G C

I have frequently been asked to define this magical thing called talent, which everyone is looking out for. I believe it is best described as natural skill plus imagination – the latter being the most difficult quality to assess. And it has a lot to do with the person's courage and their belief in what they are doing and the way they are putting it across.

4 | A ✓

Where does the desire to act come from? It is often very difficult to put into words your own reasons for wanting to act. Certainly, in the theatre the significant thing is that moment of contact between the actor on the stage and a particular audience. And making this brief contact is central to all acting, wherever it takes place – it is what drives all actors to act.

5 | F ✓

If you ask actors how they have done well in the profession, the response will most likely be a shrug. They will not know. They will know certain things about themselves and aspects of their own technique and the techniques of others. But they will take nothing for granted, because they know that they are only as good as their current job, and that their fame may not continue.

6 | D H

Disappointment is the greatest enemy of the actor. Last month you may have been out of work, selling clothes or waitressing. Suddenly you are asked to audition for a part, but however much you want the job, the truth is that it may be denied you. So actors tend not to talk about their chances. They come up with ways of protecting themselves against the stress of competing for a part and the possibility of rejection.

7 | H B

Nobody likes being rejected. And remember that the possibility is there from the very first moment you start going in for parts professionally. You are saying that you are available, willing and, hopefully, talented enough for the job. And, in many ways, it's up to you, for if you don't care enough, no-one will care for you.

3 +5 +10 = 18/35.

51%.

Part 2

You are going to read a magazine interview with a young model. For questions **8-15**, choose the answer (**A**, **B**, **C** or **D**) which you think fits best according to the text.

Mark your answers **on the separate answer sheet**.

The Schoolgirl Model

When 15-year-old Kira Langer is not flying off to wonderful locations and appearing on the covers of magazines, you'll probably find her revising for her school exams. Jane Laidlaw finds out more.

'I'm afraid Kira will be a little late,' the receptionist at the agency told me. 'Oh, fine,' I said, 'no problem.' I had been trying to convince myself that all the bad things I had read about models were rubbish, but the words *difficult*, *vain* and *unintelligent* kept coming into my head. And now she was going to be late. How late? An hour? Three hours? Maybe she wouldn't come at all. What if she had decided a visit to the hairdresser's would be more fun than talking to me? If she was late, she would be rushing. She could be in an awful mood and refuse to answer my questions.

But when the winner of the *Looks* magazine supermodel competition walked in, she was smiling, relaxed and apologetic – and with her mother. Kira was not dressed in expensive-looking designer clothes but in a simple black dress and trainers. There was no sign of a selfish attitude, she was just a very friendly, very tall, very pretty girl. All models under the age of 16 must take an adult with them whenever they work, she explained, and apart from looking incredibly young, her mother was a normal mum – visibly proud of her successful daughter.

Kira gives the impression of being slightly puzzled by her new-found fame, which is understandable since it was completely unplanned. It was her older sister who decided that she should take part in the model competition. 'She saw the competition and said I should go in for it,' Kira remembers. 'I said no, but she sent some photos in anyway.' When the call came to tell her that she was a finalist, she was at school.

The achievement of being selected for the final gave Kira the confidence to go through with it and she performed perfectly. She won easily and the Select model agency in London immediately offered her work.

Kira now finds that one of the hardest things she has to do is to manage her two separate lives. But her friends and teachers have become accustomed to having a star among them. 'They're really proud of me,' she says. However, a few unkind people at her school are rude about her success. 'They say I have too high an opinion of myself.' This kind of remark must be hard for Kira to deal with, since there can't be many people as successful as her who are less self-important. But she says, 'They assume that because I've suddenly become a model, I can't stay the same. But the only thing that's changed is I've become more confident – not in a horrible way, but I'm able to stand up for myself more.'

As a busy model though, her social life is obviously affected. The Select agency can ring at any time and tell her that she is wanted for a job the next day. 'If my friends are going out together, I can't say I'll come, because I don't know what I'm doing the next day. I can't really make plans, and if I do they sometimes get broken, but my friends are good about it. They don't say, "Oh, you're always going off modelling now, you never have time for us".'

Kira has the looks, ability and support to have a fabulous career ahead of her. And not many people can say that before they even sit their school-leaving exams. I am about to finish the interview with the girl who has it all, and I ask what she would like to do as a career if she didn't have the outstanding beauty that seems certain to take her to the top of the profession. She pauses and replies: 'I'd like to do what you're doing.'

8   Before she went to the interview with Kira, the writer
   A   was unsure what questions to ask her.
   B   was aware that Kira might be late.
   C   did not expect to like Kira.
   D   was afraid that Kira would dislike her.

9   When Kira walked in, the writer was surprised because
   A   Kira was not as attractive as she had expected.
   B   Kira did not seem to have been affected by success.
   C   Kira looked younger than she had expected.
   D   Kira apologised for her mother being there.

10   When Kira refused to enter the supermodel competition, her sister
   A   understood her feelings.
   B   lost her temper.
   C   paid no attention.
   D   tried to persuade her.

11   What does 'it' in line 38 refer to?
   A   winning the final
   B   taking part in the final
   C   enjoying success
   D   getting a career as a model

12   What does Kira think about reactions to her success at school?
   A   She feels that some criticisms of her behaviour are correct.
   B   She realises why some people are critical of her.
   C   She thinks that people are paying too much attention to her.
   D   She expects people to start treating her differently soon.

13   What does Kira say about her social life?
   A   She sometimes wishes it could carry on as before.
   B   She regrets having so little free time.
   C   She likes to accept invitations.
   D   She has some understanding friends.

14   What do we learn about Kira in the last paragraph?
   A   She doesn't expect to be a model for long.
   B   She is already thinking of a new career.
   C   She wouldn't mind becoming a journalist.
   D   She may not take her school exams.

15   The writer's view of Kira is that she is
   A   modest.
   B   lucky.
   C   ambitious.
   D   proud.

Part 3

You are going to read an extract from a magazine article about underwater exploration. Eight sentences have been removed from the extract. Choose from the sentences **A-I** the one which fits each gap (**16-22**). There is one extra sentence which you do not need to use. There is an example at the beginning (**0**).

Mark your answers **on the separate answer sheet**.

In hot water

Rachel Mills is a scientist who spends as much time as she can at the bottom of the Atlantic Ocean.

Rachel Mills teaches and does research into marine geochemistry, which means she studies the chemical processes happening in the sea. **0** **I** When she isn't teaching, she lowers herself into a steel vehicle, a vessel for underwater exploration the size of a small car, and dives three kilometres down into the Atlantic Ocean to study underwater volcanoes.

'Inside,' she says, 'space is so limited that I can reach out and touch the two pilots. **16** A dive can last for 16 hours – three hours to reach the ocean floor, ten hours gathering samples of rock and water and then three hours to get back up to the surface again.'

'If anything happens, and you have a problem and have to get to the top quickly, you can hit a panic button. The outside drops away leaving a small circular escape

vessel that gets released, and it's like letting go of a ping-pong ball in the bath – it goes rapidly to the surface. **17**

'I didn't know how I was going to react the first time I climbed into the vehicle. It was on the deck of a ship and I got in with an instructor. **18** They were testing me to see how I would react to being in such a small place.'

Now Rachel has made six dives. Last year she dived with a Russian crew. 'We went to a site which was a five-day sail west of the Canary Islands in the Atlantic. **19** It is where the Atlantic Ocean comes alive. The Russian team were dropping off some scientific equipment there to discover the effect of a multi-national programme that would make a hole 150 metres through a volcano.'

When she isn't at sea, Rachel is in her office at the Oceanography Centre, Southampton. 'Two thirds of my salary comes from teaching, which I love, but I do it so I can get on with my research into the "black smokers". This is just another name for underwater volcanoes – water comes out of the rock and turns into what looks like black smoke. **20** D A G

'The only time I've been frightened is when I first went down with the Americans. We were towing equipment on a 50-metre rope when suddenly there was an explosion.

There was this immense bang as the shock waves hit our vehicle and I thought, "I'm going to die." We stared at each other in silence, waiting. **21** HF The relief was incredible – we were still alive!'

'It's such an adventure diving down to the deepest part of the ocean. Every time I look out of the porthole and see those chimneys, there is such a sense of wonder. **22** F B I had studied the black smokers for three years for my Ph.D. When I got down there and saw them for real it was such an amazing feeling.'

A Here, on the ocean floor, is a huge area of underwater volcanoes, their chimneys all blowing out black smoke.

B Here I am on the bottom of the sea, and no-one else on this planet has ever before seen them.

C No-one's tested it yet, but I don't think it would be a very pleasant journey.

D He then talked me through the emergency procedures; including what to do if the pilot had a heart attack!

E They are used to these conditions, which mean we can't stand up or move and we must stay inside until someone opens the door from the outside.

F When it didn't happen, we couldn't believe it.

G This pours out at a rate of one metre per second and at a temperature of 350 degrees.

H After that, as you get really deep, it's near freezing point so you need a sweater, thick socks, gloves and a woolly hat.

I She is a lecturer at the Oceanography Centre at Southampton University.

Part 4

You are going to read a magazine article about some successful children and their mothers. For questions **23-35**, choose from the people (**A-F**). The people may be chosen more than once. When more than one answer is required, these may be given in any order. There is an example at the beginning (**0**).

Mark your answers **on the separate answer sheet**.

Which of the people

is guided by her parents?

0	C

says she must not neglect her physical condition?

23	E (A)

doesn't feel the need to pay attention all the time?

24	E

realise people can't be forced to do what they don't want to?

25	B	26	F

recognises the mistakes some parents make?

27	F (B)

has to make an effort when she doesn't want to?

28	E F

mentions the financial sacrifices necessary?

29	D

is pleased by the way her daughter's character has developed?

30	B

like the atmosphere at competitions?

31	A	32	C

have set themselves specific goals in their activities?

33	A	34	C

doesn't share her daughter's enthusiasm for the activity?

35	B (F)

Thrills and bills

If there's one thing guaranteed to send tears running down your cheeks, it's the sight of a brilliant child collecting a medal. Julia Gregson asked three young stars, and their mothers, to describe some of the pleasures and pains of their lives.

A ANNIKA REEDER 15, won a gold medal for gymnastics at the Commonwealth Games. Her ambitions are to become a physiotherapist and compete at the next Olympics. 'The work is very hard at the moment. There is no time to watch television, or go out with friends or do much more than gym and school. I try to take the training day by day, and when I feel very, very tired sometimes my coach gives me a day off, but usually I just carry on – you can't take too many days off, it makes you stiff.'

B ANNIKA'S MOTHER 'From an early age Annika showed tremendous potential. I've seen some parents try to push their children and it doesn't work. To perform at the level Annika does is so demanding of time and energy you have to want to do it yourself. People tell me all the time that we, as parents, have given up so much, but what they don't see is what the sport's given us. We love it and what it's done for Annika. Before she did gym she was a very shy little girl who sucked her thumb and hid behind me, but now she's met people from all over the world and she's got the confidence of success.'

C SARAH STOKES made her first show-jumping appearance at ten. Since then she has won the British National Championship. 'It's a good job my mum and dad like show-jumping because they train me and have to take me everywhere in the horse box. The shows are from one day to five days long. I don't ever get tired of it – I love show-jumping events, they are exciting and fun. Even if I didn't have Mum and Dad, I would do it because I am so determined. I'm glad they are happy when I win, but I'm not doing it for them. My goal this year is to qualify for the British young riders (under-18) team. My really big ambition is to win a gold medal at the Olympics.'

D SARAH'S MOTHER 'From the moment Sarah sat on a horse, age 1, that was it, her passion. When she was 5, she used to get up before us all to exercise her pony. To qualify for major shows you have to jump all over England. To save money, we sleep in the living quarters of our horse box. Sarah is well organised. She is 100% happy on a horse, she knows what she's doing. Watching your child succeed at something they love is hard to beat.'

E JANE McSHANE 10, is Britain's Under-14 Chess Champion. 'It's really friendly at tournaments. I know everybody and it's fun. When I'm playing, I don't concentrate. I should do really, but instead I just stare around and don't bother to think. I'm not scared of getting big-headed, I don't talk about my success at school. I don't like embarrassment.'

F JANE'S MOTHER 'Jane played her first game when she was 5. My father said, "Let's see if she likes it." My father had tried to teach me when I was young and I used to sit there bored, but Jane loved it from the start. By the end of that afternoon she had memorised all the moves, and by 6 was starting to beat adults. When she's won of course I'm pleased, but if she said she wanted to give it all up tomorrow, I wouldn't stand in her way. On the other hand I don't want to do the awful thing of putting somebody down because they are exceptional. If she has this gift, let her fulfil her potential.'

PAPER 2   WRITING (1 hour 30 minutes)

Part 1

You **must** answer this question.

1   You are staying in Britain and next weekend you are going cycling with your friends
Pete and Chris. Below is a letter which Pete has sent you with his suggestions for the
trip. You have found some information about the area, which includes a map and an
advertisement for the Lakeside Inn.

Read Pete's letter, on which you have made some notes, and the information
below it. Then write a suitable reply, answering his questions and making suggestions
about accommodation.

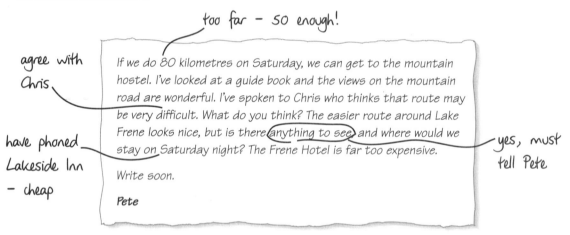

too far – so enough!

agree with Chris

have phoned Lakeside Inn – cheap

If we do 80 kilometres on Saturday, we can get to the mountain
hostel. I've looked at a guide book and the views on the mountain
road are wonderful. I've spoken to Chris who thinks that route may
be very difficult. What do you think? The easier route around Lake
Frene looks nice, but is there anything to see and where would we
stay on Saturday night? The Frene Hotel is far too expensive.

Write soon.

Pete

yes, must tell Pete

The Lakeside Inn

*Small, friendly inn. Beautiful views of
Lake Frene. Bed and breakfast, good
selection of bar food lunchtimes
and evenings.*

Reservations tel. 01967 41294

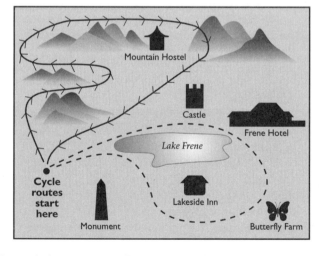

Write a **letter** to Pete of between **120** and **180** words in an appropriate style on the
opposite page. Do not write any addresses.

20-05-04

Visual materials for Paper 5

1A

PRIMARY

SECONDARY

1B

TRADITIONAL EDUCATION SYSTEM.

2A

2B

1C

1D

2C

2D

1E

2E

LOST PROPERTY

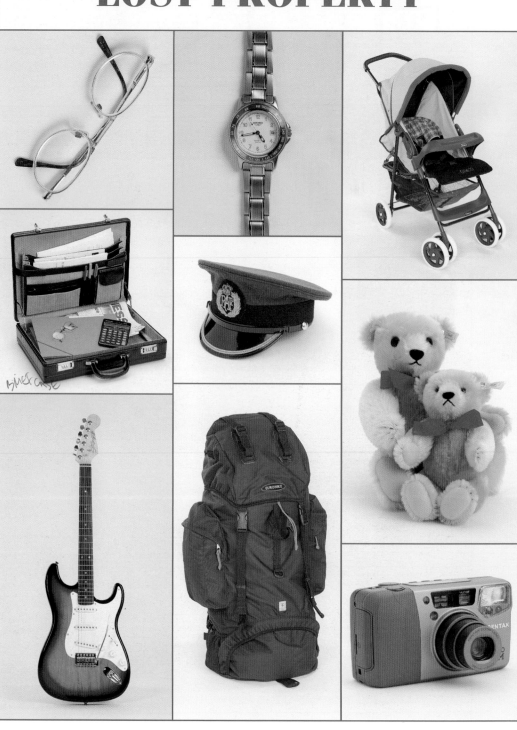

3A

3B

4A

4B

3C

3D

4C

4D

3E

freedom
speed
comfort
cost
adventure

4E

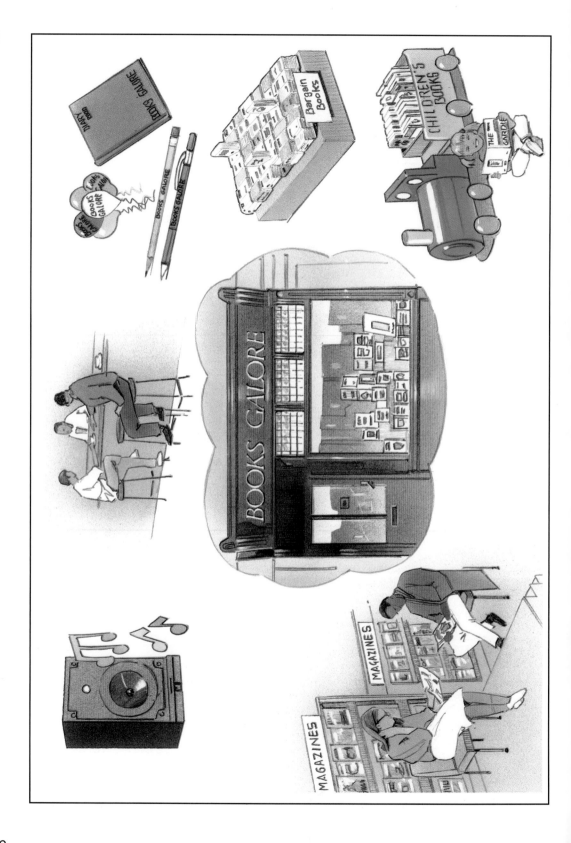

Question 1

....

....

....

....

....

....

....

....

....

....

....

....

....

....

....

....

....

....

....

....

....

....

....

....

....

....

....

....

....

....

....

....

....

Part 2

Write an answer to **one** of the questions **2-5** in this part. Write your answer in **120-180** words in an appropriate style on the opposite page. Put the question number in the box.

2   You have just read the following advertisement.

Hardworking, reliable people needed this summer for our **International Working Holiday Camp** picking fruit and vegetables

• free accommodation   • good pay • evening English course

Contact: James Felton, Whitecross Farm, Deal, Kent

Write your **letter of application** to the farm. Say why you are interested in the work and ask for more details about the information given in the advertisement. Do not write any addresses.

3   Your class has been doing a project on zoos. As part of this project, your teacher has asked you to write a composition giving your opinion on the following question:

Is there a need for zoos in the modern world?

Write your **composition**.

4   You have just returned from a visit to a museum. You have now agreed to write an article about the museum for your college magazine. Describe the museum, say what you liked or didn't like about it, and why it could be of interest to your readers.

Write your **article**.

5   Answer **one** of the following two questions based on your reading of one of these set books. Write (**a**) or (**b**) as well as the number **5** in the question box, and the **title** of the book next to the box.
Great Expectations – Charles Dickens
Crime Never Pays – Oxford Bookworms Collection
Rebecca – Daphne du Maurier
The Old Man and the Sea – Ernest Hemingway
Tales of Mystery and Imagination – Edgar Allan Poe

   Either (**a**) In the book or in one of the short stories you have read, did the main characters deserve what happened to them? Write a **composition**, giving your views.

   Or   (**b**) Choose a place or a building that plays an important part in the book or one of the short stories you have read. Write a **composition** describing the place or building and explaining its importance.

Question

....
....
....
....
....
....
....
....
....
....
....
....
....
....
....
....
....
....
....
....
....
....
....
....
....
....
....
....
....
....
....
....
....

PAPER 3   USE OF ENGLISH (1 hour 15 minutes)

Part 1

For questions **1-15** read the text below and decide which answer (**A**, **B**, **C** or **D**) best fits each space. There is an example at the beginning (**0**).
Mark your answers **on the separate answer sheet**.

Example:

0   A   expanded   **B**   swollen   **C**   widened   **D**   stretched

```
0 | A   B   C   D
    _   _   _   _
```

THE PATHÉ FILM COMPANY

In 1885, a Frenchman, Charles Pathé, created what later became France's most successful film studios. By 1907, the company had **(0)** ..... enormously and had studios in France, Britain, Germany, Italy, Spain and the USA. What seems surprising now that Hollywood dominates the film **(1)** ..... is that a French company **(2)** ..... itself so well in the USA. Pathé was one of the main film companies there at that **(3)** ..... , hiring out its studios to other film-making companies **(4)** ..... distributing its own films.

However, **(5)** ..... Pathé was big in the USA, it was a giant in Europe. In 1913, the year before the First World War **(6)** ..... , Pathé made no fewer than three hundred films. But the war affected the company **(7)** ..... . Shortages of staff and equipment led to big **(8)** ..... in production, and by 1918 output had **(9)** ..... to sixty-three films. From then on, Pathé **(10)** ..... on making fewer films of **(11)** ..... length and better quality.

Pathé was the first company to put out regular news films, which it started doing in 1903. Each film lasted fifteen minutes and **(12)** ..... of six news items. From **(13)** ..... on, Pathé's news department had branches all over Europe and later all over the world. By the 1970s, TV news had completely **(14)** ..... the role of cinema news films and so the company stopped making them. Today, Pathé is chiefly **(15)** ..... in TV, cinema and new video technology.

1   **A** life   **B** world   **C** area   **D** channel

2   **A** established   **B** set   **C** founded   **D** placed

3   **A** date   **B** phase   **C** age   **D** time

4   **A** in addition   **B** together   **C** as well as   **D** also

5   **A** so   **B** whether   **C** despite   **D** if

6   **A** burst out   **B** broke out   **C** set off   **D** went off

7   **A** badly   **B** extremely   **C** largely   **D** highly

8   **A** chops   **B** slips   **C** cuts   **D** dips

9   **A** descended   **B** shortened   **C** fallen   **D** subtracted

10 **A** thought   **B** engaged   **C** occupied   **D** concentrated

11 **A** further   **B** greater   **C** higher   **D** bigger

12 **A** consisted   **B** featured   **C** included   **D** composed

13 **A** soon   **B** firstly   **C** early   **D** initially

14 **A** brought off   **B** turned into   **C** caught on   **D** taken over

15 **A** involved   **B** connected   **C** linked   **D** tied

Part 2

For questions **16-30**, read the text below and think of the word which best fits each space. Use only **one** word in each space. There is an example at the beginning (**0**). Write your answers **on the separate answer sheet**.

Example: | **0** | in |

THE LONDON MARATHON

The London Marathon is one of the best-known long-distance races (**0**) ....in.... the world. Some of the (**16**) .... famous long-distance runners have competed in it. But (**17**) .... makes it different from many other great sporting events is (**18**) .... fact that ordinary people can (**19**) .... part alongside international stars.

The race was the idea of Chris Brasher, a former Olympic athlete. In 1979, friends told him about the New York Marathon, during (**20**) .... the runners are encouraged to carry (**21**) .... to the end of the course by the enthusiastic shouts of the spectators. He flew to the USA to run in the race (**22**) .... was so impressed by (**23**) .... that he decided to organise a similar event in Britain. Many problems (**24**) .... to be overcome before the first London Marathon took place in 1981. Chris Brasher still takes a keen interest in the event, even though he is no (**25**) .... the organiser.

(**26**) .... total of around 300,000 runners have completed the race, with a record of 25,194 finishing in 1984. Numbers are limited (**27**) .... the streets of London are too narrow to accommodate all those (**28**) .... would like to run. Each year more than 70,000 apply (**29**) .... the 26,000 places in the race. Hundreds of thousands of spectators line the route and at least a hundred countries televise it. Over the years, (**30**) .... the first race was held, an estimated £75 million has been raised for charity by the runners.

Part 3

For questions **31–40**, complete the second sentence so that it has a similar meaning to the first sentence, using the word given. **Do not change the word given**. You must use between **two** and **five** words, including the word given.

Here is an example (**0**).

Example:

0   You must do exactly what the manager tells you.

carry

You must .... instructions exactly.

The gap can be filled by the words 'carry out the manager's' so you write:

0	carry out the manager's

Write **only** the missing words **on the separate answer sheet**.

---

31   The fire in the library was discovered by a student.

who

It .... the fire in the library.

32   Gerald is too young to vote.

old

Gerald .... vote.

33   'Do fast cars interest you?' the dealer asked Sarah.

was

The dealer asked Sarah .... fast cars.

34   My brother really wishes he could sing well.

able

My brother regrets not .... well.

35 Maria said I had caused the accident.

blamed

Maria .... the accident.

36 James did not need to register for the new course.

necessary

It .... to register for the new course.

37 She never finishes her work on time although she works hard.

matter

She never finishes her work on time .... she
works.

38 There haven't been many changes in this town since I last visited it.

much

Since my last .... has changed in this town.

39 Hardly anybody applied for the job.

applicants

There were very .... the job.

40 Luisa does a full-time job and looks after the house too.

well

Luisa does a full-time job .... the house.

Part 4

For questions **41-55**, read the text below and look carefully at each line. Some of the lines are correct, and some have a word which should not be there.

If a line is correct, put a tick (✓) by the number **on the separate answer sheet**. If a line has a word which should **not** be there, write the word **on the separate answer sheet**. There are two examples at the beginning (**0** and **00**).

Examples:

0	✓
00	being

A HOLIDAY DISAPPOINTMENT

0	Things started to go wrong as soon as we got to
00	the hotel. We were all being completely exhausted after
41	our long journey and looking forward to have a shower
42	and a rest. However, we found that our room was yet not
43	ready, which was very much annoying, although the manager
44	was extremely apologetic. While we were waiting, we asked
45	about the excursions to places of an interest which we had
46	read about them in the brochure. Imagine how we felt when
47	we were told they had all been cancelled away! Apparently,
48	the person who responsible for organising them had left
49	suddenly and had not been replaced. Then Sally saw a
50	notice that pinned to the door of the restaurant, saying
51	it was been closed for redecoration, and Peter discovered that
52	the swimming pool it was empty. When we eventually got
53	to our room we were horrified to so find that it was at the
54	back of the hotel, and we had a view out of a car park, which
55	seemed to be used as a rubbish dump. We seriously began to
	wonder whether or not to stay.

Part 5

For questions **56-65**, read the text below. Use the word given in capitals at the end of each line to form a word that fits in the space in the same line. There is an example at the beginning (**0**). Write your answers **on the separate answer sheet**.

Example: | **0** | *following* |

WORRIES ABOUT A FACTORY

There is considerable public concern in Shaston (**0**) *following*	**FOLLOW**
the discovery on Tuesday evening of a metal (**56**) ..... filled	**CONTAIN**
with (**57**) ..... liquid. The object was found by a local	**POISON**
(**58**) ..... walking his dog in a field behind a newly-built	**RESIDE**
chemical factory. As yet, the factory has been (**59**) ..... to	**ABLE**
provide any (**60**) ..... as to how the object came to be in the	**EXPLAIN**
field. A spokesperson stated that a full (**61**) ..... was taking	**INVESTIGATE**
place and that (**62**) ..... procedures were being reviewed.	**SECURE**
People living in the (**63**) ..... are angry, as a year ago they had	**NEIGHBOUR**
withdrawn their objections to the (**64**) ..... to build the factory	**DECIDE**
here after the company stated that no (**65**) ..... chemicals	**DANGER**
would be produced on this site.	

PAPER 4   LISTENING (approximately 40 minutes)

Part 1

You will hear people talking in eight different situations. For questions **1-8**, choose the best answer, **A**, **B** or **C**.

---

1 Listen to these students discussing a book.
What do the students think of the book?

   A It has an unsatisfactory ending.

   B There are too many characters in it.

   C It is better in the original language.

1

2 Listen to this woman making a telephone call.
Why has she phoned?

   A to ask for a lift

   B to explain her plans

   C to arrange a meeting

2

3 You turn on the radio and hear part of a programme.
What type of programme is it?

   A the news

   B a documentary

   C a film review

3

4 You hear part of a radio interview.
What do we find out about the woman?

   A She is planning a journey.

   B She is doing research.

   C She is travelling with her family.

4

5 You overhear this conversation in a college corridor.
What does the man say about the lecture?

   A It's important.

   B It's been cancelled.

   C It will be held next week.

	5

6 Listen to this woman talking to her friend.
Where has she been?

   A to the doctor's

   B to the chemist's

   C to the dentist's

	6

7 You overhear two people talking about a holiday one of them has just had.
How did the woman feel?

   A relaxed

   B pleased

   C disappointed

	7

8 Listen to this woman talking to a group.
Who is she talking to?

   A people living in rented property

   B agencies that let property

   C owners of property

	8

Part 2

You will hear part of a radio programme about public transport in cities, using rickshaws – carts drawn by a bicycle. For questions **9-18**, complete the sentences.

Grabner's rickshaws come from [**9**]

The Berlin service runs during the [**10**] season.

It has expanded from a total of 400 customers

in its first year to 400 [**11**]

At first, people thought Grabner was rather [**12**]

He sometimes felt that the business might be a [**13**]

The drivers are [**14**] and other people needing extra income.

They charge passengers about $14 for a [**15**] journey.

Drivers can make up to ten journeys a day if there is [**16**]

Berlin has cycle lanes and small [**17**] especially for bikes.

A similar scheme in Britain was opposed by [**18**]

Part 3

You will hear five people talking about their favourite holiday destinations. For questions **19-23**, choose from the list **A-F** what each speaker says about the place. Use the letters only once. There is one extra letter which you do not need to use.

A It is their own property.

Speaker 1   19

B They are careful to preserve its environment.

Speaker 2   20

C The journey there is not an easy one.

Speaker 3   21

D It has always been popular with the British.

Speaker 4   22

E They would like to live there permanently.

Speaker 5   23

F It is easy to make friends with the local inhabitants.

Part 4

You will hear an interview with someone who works in the film industry. For questions
24-30, choose the best answer, **A**, **B** or **C**.

24   What does Alan say about his job title?

    A   It confuses a lot of people.

    B   It is just a name for the job.

    C   It encourages him to work hard.

                                                                                  24

25   Alan considers his job to be

    A   creative.

    B   managerial.

    C   administrative.

                                                                                      25

26   When he started in films, Alan

    A   immediately learnt new skills.

    B   did the same kind of work as before.

    C   had to change his working methods.

                                                                                 26

27   When Alan was working on his latest film,

    A   problems were caused by the weather.

    B   there were difficulties moving the equipment.

    C   he wished he was in the studio.

                                                                                27

28   For Alan, the disadvantage of the job is

    A   the amount of responsibility.

    B   the criticism he receives.

    C   the effect on family life.

                                                                                 28

29   For a job like this, Alan recommends

    A   studying to be an electrician.

    B   getting a qualification in maths.

    C   doing a course in film production.

                                                                                 29

30   In thinking about the future, Alan wants to

    A   face different problems.

    B   work in other areas of production.

    C   continue doing the same job.

                                                                                 30

PAPER 5   SPEAKING (14 minutes)

You take the Speaking test with another candidate, referred to here as your partner. There are two examiners. One will speak to you and your partner and the other will be listening. Both examiners will award marks.

Part 1 (3 minutes)

The examiner asks you and your partner questions about yourselves. You may be asked about things like 'your home town', 'your interests', 'your career plans', etc.

Part 2 (4 minutes)

The examiner gives you two photographs and asks you to talk about them for one minute. The examiner then asks your partner a question about your photographs and your partner responds briefly.

Then the examiner gives your partner two different photographs. Your partner talks about these photographs for one minute. This time the examiner asks you a question about your partner's photographs and you respond briefly.

Part 3 (3 minutes)

The examiner asks you and your partner to talk together. You may be asked to solve a problem or try to come to a decision about something. For example, you might be asked to decide the best way to use some rooms in a language school. The examiner gives you a picture to help you but does not join in the conversation.

Part 4 (4 minutes)

The examiner joins in the conversation. You all talk together in a more general way about what has been said in Part 3. The examiner asks you questions but you and your partner are also expected to develop the conversation.

Test 4

PAPER 1   READING (1 hour 15 minutes)

Part 1

You are going to read a newspaper article about climbing. Choose from the list **A-I** the most suitable heading for each part (**1-7**) of the article. There is one extra heading which you do not need to use. There is an example at the beginning (**0**).

Mark your answers **on the separate answer sheet**.

A	Early imperfections
B	Something in common
C	The demand for indoor practice
D	Useful attachments
E	Indoor climbing is preferred
F	The inventor of the wall
G	Putting up with nature
H	A lighter construction method
I	Watching the expert

07.05-05

Going up the wall

Once climbers went to the mountains. Now a challenging climb can be had anywhere, indoors or out.

0 | **I**

The crowd holds its breath. High above them on the climbing wall, hanging upside down by the tips of two fingers, is the French climber François Lombard. He is competing in the World Cup Climbing Championships at Birmingham's National Indoor Arena.

1 | B

The National Indoor Arena is more famous for staging the TV show Gladiators, but the television programme and the World Cup Climbing Championships share at least one feature – The Wall. And the fact that either event is possible is the result of a new and rapidly developing technology.

2 | G

Until the mid-1960s, climbers practised their skills on cliffs in areas where there was a plentiful supply of good climbing angles. During the winter they would either tolerate the cold weather, go walking instead or climb on snow and ice in Scotland.

3 | A C

However, as the sport developed it was increasingly important for top climbers to keep fit. With the cliffs unusable for much of the year, they used brick-edges or stone buildings to 'work out' on. This allowed them to keep their fingers strong, and beat off the boredom of not being able to climb. It wasn't long before many sports centres started building walls specifically for the task, using bricks with special edges to cling on to.

4 | F

Many of these early walls followed the example set by Don Robinson, a teacher of physical education who, during the mid-1960s, constructed a climbing wall in a corridor of his department at Leeds University. Robinson developed the idea of setting natural rock in a block of concrete, which could then be included in a wall.

5 | A

Scores of climbing walls of this kind were built in sports halls up and down the country throughout the 1970s but they had obvious design problems. Walls could only be built in a vertical plane, whereas cliffs outside have features like overhangs and angled slabs of rock. There was the added drawback that once the walls were up they couldn't be altered and climbers would eventually tire of their repetitive nature, despite thinking of every combination of holds possible.

6 | D

In 1985, a Frenchman, François Savigny, developed a material which he moulded into shapes like those that climbers would find on the cliffs. These could be fixed onto any existing wall and then taken off when climbers got bored with a particular combination.

7 | H

French manufacturers also began to experiment with panels on a steel framework. Concrete had proved too heavy to create overhanging walls without major building work, but steel frames could be erected anywhere as free-standing structures. A system of interchangeable fixtures gave climbers an endless supply of new holds.

Part 2

You are going to read an extract from a short story. For questions **8-14**, choose the answer (**A, B, C** or **D**) which you think fits best according to the text.

Mark your answers **on the separate answer sheet**.

In the <u>lumberyard</u> by the lake, where trees from the woods were turned into boards for construction work, there was an old brick building two floors high, and all around the outside walls were heaped great piles of soft <u>sawdust</u>. There were many of these golden mountains of dust covering that part of the yard right down to the blue lake. That afternoon, bored with having nothing else to do, all the fellows followed Michael up the ladder to the roof of the old building and they sat with their legs hanging over the edge looking out across the lake. Suddenly Michael said, 'I <u>dare</u> you to jump down,' and without thinking about it, he pushed himself off the roof and fell on the <u>sawdust</u> where he lay rolling around and laughing. 'I dare you all!' he shouted. 'You're all <u>cowards</u>,' he said, encouraging them to follow him. Still laughing, he watched them looking down from the roof, white-faced and hesitant, and then one by one they jumped and got up grinning with relief.

In the hot afternoon sunlight they all lay on the sawdust pile telling jokes till at last one of the fellows said, 'Come on up on the old roof again and jump down.' There wasn't much enthusiasm among them, but they all went up to the roof again and began to jump off in a determined, desperate way till only Michael was left and the others were all down below <u>grinning up at him</u> calling, 'Come on, Mike. What's the matter with you?' Michael wanted to jump down there and be with them, but he remained on the edge of the roof, wetting his lips, with a silly grin on his face, wondering why it had not seemed such a long drop the first time. For a while they thought he was only <u>fooling</u> them, but then they saw him <u>clenching</u> his <u>fists</u> tight. He was trying to count to ten and then jump, and when that failed, he tried to take a long breath and close his eyes. In a while the fellows began to laugh at him; they were tired of waiting and it was getting on to dinnertime. 'Come on, you're a coward, do you think we're going to sit here all night?' they began to shout, and when he did not move they began to get up and walk away, still shouting. 'Who did this in the first place? What's the matter with you all?' he called.

But for a long time he remained on the edge of the roof, staring unhappily and steadily at the ground. He remained all alone for nearly an hour while the sun, like a great orange ball getting bigger and bigger, rolled slowly over the grey line beyond the lake. His clothes were wet from nervous sweating. At last he closed his eyes, slipped off the roof, fell heavily on the pile of sawdust and lay there a long time. There were no sounds in the yard, the workmen had gone home. As he lay there he wondered why he had been unable to jump; and then he got up slowly and walked home feeling deeply ashamed and wanting to avoid everybody.

He was so late for dinner that his stepmother said to him coldly, 'You're big enough by this time surely to be able to get home in time for dinner. But if you won't come home, you'd better try staying in tonight.' She was a well-built woman with a fair, soft skin and a little touch of grey in her hair and an eternally patient smile on her face. She was speaking now with a controlled severity, but Michael, with his dark face gloomy and miserable, hardly heard her; he was still seeing the row of grinning faces down below on the sawdust pile and hearing them laugh at him.

8 Why did the boys first climb on the building?

    A to test their courage

    B to pass the time

    C to keep out of the way of the workmen

    D to get a better view of the woods

9 When the boys jumped after Michael, they

    A were grateful to him for the idea.

    B wanted to do it again immediately.

    C felt pleased at what they had done.

    D found the jump harder than expected.

10 Why didn't Michael make the second jump immediately?

    A The ground seemed further away.

    B He thought his friends had been foolish.

    C He was trying to trick his friends.

    D He wanted something to drink.

11 How did Michael's friends react when he didn't jump?

    A They left immediately.

    B They were not surprised.

    C They remembered how they had felt themselves.

    D They thought he was joking.

12 When Michael finally jumped the second time, he

    A was proud of himself.

    B improved on his first jump.

    C could not understand what had stopped him.

    D was not so angry with his friends.

13 When his stepmother criticised his behaviour, Michael

    A wished he had come home earlier.

    B was thinking about something else.

    C had not expected her to behave like this.

    D was glad she was a patient woman.

14 What is the writer trying to do in this text?

    A describe a difficult experience in Michael's life

    B show how children can work together

    C show the dangers of life in the countryside

    D describe Michael's fear of his family

Part 3

You are going to read a magazine article about a girl and the job she does. Eight sentences have been removed from the article. Choose from the sentences **A-I** the one which fits each gap (**15-21**). There is one extra sentence which you do not need to use. There is an example at the beginning (**0**).

Mark your answers **on the separate answer sheet**.

Keeping the holiday-makers happy

A chalet girl's work is never done, Sarah Sutherland-Pilch tells Veronica Lee – in between making beds and delicious dinners.

This is the second year as a chalet girl for Sarah Sutherland-Pilch, a 24-year-old from West Sussex. Known by her nickname, Pilch, Sarah works for a company in Val d'Isère, France, cooking and cleaning for visitors who come to ski and stay in the wooden houses, known as chalets, that are characteristic of the area. Sarah graduated in French and History of Art from Oxford Brookes University last summer. **0** **I** 'It's a good way to make contacts. I meet successful people every week.'

Sarah does not 'live in'. **15** **A** She has her own breakfast before preparing that of the guests. 'They get the works – porridge, eggs, cereals, fruit and croissants.' When the last of the guests has had breakfast, by about 9.30 a.m., Sarah clears up and either makes the afternoon tea, which is left for the guests to help themselves, or cleans the rooms – 'the worst part of the job,' she says.

By about 11 a.m. she is ready to go on the slopes herself. She skis as much as possible. **16** **F** Sarah returns to the chalet in time to prepare dinner and takes a shower before doing so, but does not sleep. 'It's fatal if you do,' she says.

Dinner, a three-course affair, is served at 8 p.m. and coffee is usually on the table by 10 p.m. Sarah clears away the dinner things and fills the dishwasher. **17** **B** Sometimes she will stay and chat with the guests, other times they are content to be left alone. 'Good guests can make a week brilliant – breakfast this morning was great fun – but some weeks, for whatever reason, don't go quite so well.'

Sarah meets her friends in the chalet where she lives – and they go out at about 11 p.m. 'We usually start off in *Bananas*, might go to *G Jay's* and perhaps *Dick's T-Bar* at the end of the evening,' she says. But Sarah never stays out too late on Saturday night as Sunday is her busiest time of the week. **18** H ~~F~~

Work begins earlier than usual on Sunday, since breakfast for guests who are leaving has to be on the table by 7 a.m. **19** C 'We just blitz the place – clear the breakfast, strip the beds, get everything ready.' If she hasn't already done the week's shop on Saturday, Sarah does it now.

20 D A 'They get here at around 4.30 p.m. Sometimes they are disorientated and full of questions. I'm sure it's the mountain air that does something to them.'

Between tea and dinner, Sarah takes any guests needing boots or skis down to the ski shop and then gets a lift back to the chalet from one of the ski shop staff. **21** E H 'Sometimes I'm so tired I just have an early night,' she says.

A At around 3 p.m., the cleaning work done, Sarah then prepares tea for the new guests.

B Sarah enjoys cooking and, after leaving school, supported herself during holidays by working as a cook.

C 'There's nothing worse than coming in to a messy kitchen the next morning.'

D As soon as the guests are gone, Sarah starts cleaning madly.

E 'On a good day we can be up there until 4.30 p.m.'

F 'A frightful day,' she says, 'when you certainly don't want to be cooking breakfast with a terrible headache.'

G She gets up at 7 a.m. to walk the mile or so to the chalet, which sleeps up to 18 guests each week.

H It is soon time for dinner duty again and perhaps a drink later, but not always.

I Being a chalet girl isn't a career, she says, but an enjoyable way to spend a year or two before settling down.

Part 4

You are going to read a magazine article about five orchestral conductors. For questions **22-35**, choose from the conductors (**A-E**). The conductors may be chosen more than once. When more than one answer is required, these may be given in any order. There is an example at the beginning (**0**).

Mark your answers **on the separate answer sheet**.

Which conductor or conductors …

has an open mind about the work he/she accepts?	**0**	**D**	
did not plan to become a conductor?	**22**	*D*	*A,E*
have had difficulties with other performers?	**23**	*C*	**24** *E*
talks about the problems of getting suitable work?	**25**	*B*	
enjoys the preparation for a performance?	**26**	*C*	
have had no professional training as conductors?	**27**	*A*	**28** *E*
had an unexpected experience early in their careers?	**29**	*A*	**30** *E*
is glad he/she did not succeed sooner?	**31**	*D*	
received help from a national organisation?	**32**	*A*	
created his/her own musical company?	**33**	*D*	
mentions a possible danger he/she faces?	**34**	*B*	
thinks it is essential to appear confident?	**35**	*E*	

Conduct becoming

Giving directions to an orchestra is never easy. Anne Inglis talks to five new conductors about their work.

A ANNE MANSON

When Anne Manson, 30, asked if she could attend conductor Claudio Abbado's practice sessions in Vienna, she found herself standing in for an absent assistant. She was then asked to help on another opera the next season. 'I had to take the first orchestral rehearsal for Abbado. No, I wasn't nervous. I always had a good attitude to standing up in front of an orchestra.' American-born Manson works with a well established London-based opera company which concentrates on modern works. She is also building a reputation in other European countries, which she has visited with financial aid from the British Arts Council, and, since that first occasion, she has assisted Abbado on several more projects.

B ANDREW CONSTANTINE

The most difficult part of being a conductor is deciding how to convince people to present you with the right opportunities,' says Andrew Constantine, 31, who won a major competition in 1991, after failed attempts in two other contests. Looking back, he is grateful for the timing: 'If it had happened any earlier, I am sure I would have disappeared without trace.' The competition provided many performance opportunities and a period as assistant to a well-known conductor, but Constantine is finding it difficult to lose the 'competition' label: 'If in three years' time my name is still associated with the competition then I will be worried,' he says. 'But orchestras such as the English Chamber Orchestra who took me on after the competition are now inviting me back. If this doesn't happen, your career will gradually fall to pieces.'

C WASFI KANI

Wasfi Kani, who set up Pimlico Opera, loves the long practice period which is part of any opera production. 'The music is worth four weeks' attention,' says Kani, who started conducting seriously in her late twenties. After university, she supported herself by working in London's commercial centre until Pimlico Opera turned fully professional two years ago. Starting lessons with Sian Edwards was the key moment for her. 'I saw her conduct and realised she was the same size as me – I had always been taught by much bigger people which makes a huge difference.' She likes the complicated nature of opera: 'There are lots of arguments, and you've got singers' personalities to consider ...'

D ROGER VIGNOLES

'Conducting has come upon me as something of a surprise, but it holds great fascination for me,' says Roger Vignoles, 48. In fact, it's not such a strange career move. He started out as a resident musician with an opera house, and worked with good conductors. Last year he was asked to direct Handel's *Agrippina* from the piano at a festival, something he had never done before. 'It was much less difficult than I thought. I found I knew the music well, I knew what I wanted it to sound like, and I tried my best to get the performance I wanted. Fortunately, people have respected my ability as a musician generally. I am benefiting from every piece of experience I've ever had, both in musical style and in the actual business of performing. Now I will do whatever people ask me to do so I can find out what I like doing.'

E WAYNE MARSHALL

It was back in 1986 that the conductor Simon Rattle noticed a young assistant conductor on one of his productions and told his agent about Wayne Marshall. Marshall, now 32, soon found himself conducting a musical in London at short notice, a difficult beginning. He even had to deal with some over-relaxed professional musicians reading newspapers during the show: 'I was just tough with them. I always gave a clear beat and got the best result I could. A lot of orchestral musicians I've seen don't seem to need advice and instruction from a conductor. But I'm never afraid to say what I want. If people see you're worried, it gets worse. I've never studied conducting formally and no book tells you how to conduct but people have been kind to me. I am determined and I know what I like.'

© *BBC Music* Jan 1994

PAPER 2   WRITING (1 hour 30 minutes)

Part 1

You **must** answer this question.

1   You help to organise meetings at your local sports club. You have written to an international sports star who is going to visit your area, inviting him to give a talk at your club. He has agreed and he has written to you asking for more information.

Read his letter, on which you have made some notes, and write a reply to him.

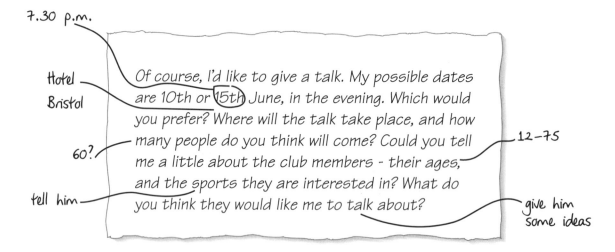

7.30 p.m.

Hotel
Bristol

60?

tell him

Of course, I'd like to give a talk. My possible dates are 10th or 15th June, in the evening. Which would you prefer? Where will the talk take place, and how many people do you think will come? Could you tell me a little about the club members - their ages, and the sports they are interested in? What do you think they would like me to talk about?

12–75

give him
some ideas

Write a **letter** of between **120** and **180** words in an appropriate style on the opposite page. Do not write any addresses.

Question 1

Part 2

Write an answer to **one** of the questions **2-5** in this part. Write your answer in **120-180** words in an appropriate style on the opposite page. Put the question number in the box.

2   You have had a class discussion on the following question:

Which are the most important subjects for young people to study at school and why?

Now your teacher has asked you to write a composition, giving your opinion on this question.

Write your **composition**.

3   You have decided to enter a short story competition. The competition rules say that the story must begin **or** end with the following sentence:

Suddenly I heard a noise behind me.

Write your **story** for the competition.

4   A group of British students would like to go camping in your area. The group leader has asked you to write a report, answering these questions:

• Where is the best place to camp in your area, and why?

• What is the best time of year for camping there?

• What clothes should the group members bring with them?

Write your **report**.

5   Answer **one** of the following two questions based on your reading of **one** of these set books. Write (**a**) or (**b**) as well as the number **5** in the question box, and the **title** of the book next to the box.

Great Expectations – Charles Dickens
Rebecca – Daphne du Maurier
Crime Never Pays – Oxford Bookworms Collection
The Old Man and the Sea – Ernest Hemingway
Tales of Mystery and Imagination – Edgar Allan Poe

Either (a)   A television company has given you the opportunity to interview one of the characters from the book you have read. Write a **letter** to the television company, telling them which character you would choose, what questions you would ask that character, and why.

Or   (b)   How successful is the ending of the book or short story you have read? Write a **composition**, briefly describing the ending and giving your opinion on how successful it is.

Question

....
....
....
....
....
....
....
....
....
....
....
....
....
....
....
....
....
....
....
....
....
....
....
....
....
....
....
....
....
....

PAPER 3 USE OF ENGLISH (1 hour 15 minutes)

Part 1

For questions **1-15**, read the text below and decide which answer (**A**, **B**, **C** or **D**) best fits each space. There is an example at the beginning (**0**).
Mark your answers **on the separate answer sheet**.

Example:

0 A planet   **B** world   **C** earth   **D** globe

```
0 | A | B | C | D
```

MARKETS

In practically any country in the **(0)** ..... , you are **(1)** ..... to find a market somewhere. Markets have been with us since **(2)** ..... times, when people became self-sufficient and needed to exchange the goods they produced. For example, a farmer might have exchanged a cow **(3)** ..... tools and so on. But just as times have **(4)** ..... , so have market practices. So, **(5)** ..... in early times the main activity **(6)** ..... with markets would have been 'bartering', meaning the exchange of goods as described **(7)** ..... , today most stall-holders wouldn't be too **(8)** ..... on accepting potatoes as payment, for instance, instead of cash.

In contrast, what might be a common **(9)** ..... in a modern market is a certain amount of 'haggling', where customer and seller eventually **(10)** ..... on a price, after what can sometimes be quite a heated debate. This has become so popular in certain places that many people think that this is what makes the **(11)** ..... atmosphere of a market. But **(12)** ..... as no two people are the same, no two markets are the same either, and so behaviour which is expected in one market in one country may not be **(13)** ..... in another. Even within one country, there are those markets where you could haggle quite **(14)** ..... and those where you would be **(15)** ..... not to try!

1   **A** safe   **B** confident   **C** definite   **D** sure

2   **A** ancient   **B** antique   **C** old   **D** past

3   **A** into   **B** by   **C** for   **D** over

4   **A** changed   **B** turned   **C** developed   **D** differed

5   **A** however   **B** despite   **C** nevertheless   **D** whereas

6   **A** associated   **B** relating   **C** connecting   **D** attached

7   **A** over   **B** above   **C** upper   **D** higher

8   **A** fond   **B** keen   **C** eager   **D** pleased

9   **A** look   **B** appearance   **C** sight   **D** view

10 **A** confirm   **B** consent   **C** approve   **D** agree

11 **A** sole   **B** single   **C** only   **D** unique

12 **A** even   **B** so   **C** just   **D** such

13 **A** acceptable   **B** convenient   **C** comfortable   **D** receptive

14 **A** simply   **B** plainly   **C** clearly   **D** easily

15 **A** informed   **B** advised   **C** noticed   **D** suggested

Part 2

For questions **16-30**, read the text below and think of the word which best fits each space. Use only **one** word in each space. There is an example at the beginning (**0**). Write your answers **on the separate answer sheet**.

Example: | **0** | *be* |

SAVING THE TIGER

In 1973, when the tiger appeared to (**0**) ...*be*.... facing extinction, the World Wide Fund for Nature and (**16**) .... Indian Government agreed to set (**17**) .... 'Operation Tiger' – a campaign (**18**) .... save this threatened creature. They started by creating nine special parks (**19**) .... that tigers could live in safety. The first was at Ranthambhore, a region (**20**) .... was quickly turning into a desert (**21**) .... too much of the grass was being eaten by the local people's cattle. At the time there (**22**) .... just fourteen tigers left there. The government had to clear twelve small villages, which meant moving nearly 1,000 people and 10,000 cattle so the land (**23**) .... be handed back to nature.

Today, Ranthambhore is a very different place, with grass tall (**24**) .... for tigers to hide in, and there are now at (**25**) .... forty of them (**26**) .... the park, wandering freely about. Other animals have also benefited. For example, there are many (**27**) .... deer and monkeys than before. The people (**28**) .... were moved are now living in better conditions. They live in new villages away (**29**) .... the tiger park, with schools, temples and fresh water supplies. There are now sixteen such tiger parks in India and the animal's future looks (**30**) .... little safer.

Part 3

For questions **31-40**, complete the second sentence so that it has a similar meaning to the first sentence, using the word given. **Do not change the word given**. You must use between **two** and **five** words, including the word given.

Here is an example (**0**).

Example:

0   You must do exactly what the manager tells you.

carry

You must .... instructions exactly.

The gap can be filled by the words 'carry out the manager's' so you write:

| **0** | *carry out the manager's* |

Write **only the missing words** on the separate answer sheet.

___

31   My grandfather was sixty when he learnt to swim.

age

My grandfather learnt to swim .... sixty.

32   Joan couldn't eat the food because it was too spicy.

too

The food .... Joan to eat.

33   It is a teacher's responsibility to look after students.

responsible

A teacher .... students.

34   It's more than a year since I saw Lucy.

for

I .... more than a year.

35 You might be late back so take a key.

case

Take a key .... late.

36 I'm sorry I didn't come to see you earlier.

wish

I .... to see you earlier.

37 People estimate that the painting is worth over a million pounds.

estimated

The painting .... over a million pounds.

38 They aren't opening that new computer shop until next week.

being

That new computer shop .... until next week.

39 'Whose is this football?' the teacher asked the children.

to

'Who .... ?' the teacher asked the children.

40 It was difficult to persuade Rick to buy the book.

difficulty

I .... Rick to buy the book.

Part 4

For questions **41-55**, read the text below and look carefully at each line. Some of the lines are correct, and some have a word which should not be there.

If a line is correct, put a tick (✓) by the number **on the separate answer sheet**. If a line has a word which should **not** be there, write the word **on the separate answer sheet**. There are two examples at the beginning (**0** and **00**).

Examples:

0	✓
00	in

A LONG WAIT

0	I thought I would let you know how much I enjoyed our holiday
00	together in last week. The only trouble with enjoying yourself as
41	much as we did is that life can seem so dull afterwards. Things
42	started to go wrong when I have got to the airport and was told
43	my flight would be delayed for at very least three hours. There was
44	really nothing to do but wait. I felt very hungry but I could
45	not buy anything to eat as I had run out of money. Time
46	passed over really slowly. After about two and a half hours there
47	was an announcement to say us that there would be a further
48	delay of up to two hours, and passengers booked on the flight
49	could order a free meal in the café. I joined up a long queue
50	and had just been being served when I heard another
51	announcement telling to passengers that the flight was now
52	ready made for boarding. I had to leave my meal and rush to the
53	gate. There was yet another wait at the gate for half of an hour
54	but we did eventually leave more than four hours late. It was not
55	a very good end to what until then had been a so fantastic holiday.

Part 5

For questions **56-65**, read the text below. Use the word given in capitals at the end of each line to form a word that fits in the space in the same line. There is an example at the beginning (**0**). Write your answers **on the separate answer sheet**.

Example:

0	*concerned*

WHAT SPOILS THE OPERA FOR ME!

As far as I am (**0**) .*concerned*. nothing spoils a visit to the opera more   **CONCERN**

than the (**56**) ..... noise made by some members of the audience to   **DISGUST**

express their (**57**) ..... of a production. There was a time when   **APPROVE**

applause, and shouts of 'bravo', were (**58**) ..... to be sufficient.   **THINK**

More (**59**) ..... , however, the practice, which I first met in the United   **RECENT**

States, of screaming 'Yo!' or something similar, has spread to (**60**) .....   **EUROPE**

audiences. It's a stupid sound, quite (**61**) ..... for the expression of   **SUIT**

your appreciation of fine (**62**) ..... like the Spaniard, Placido Domingo.   **SING**

I'm not too keen, either, on musicians clapping (**63**) ..... at   **SELF**

the end of a (**64**) ..... . They are hardly likely to be fair in their   **PERFORM**

(**65**) ..... at that moment. However, I don't imagine either of these   **JUDGE**

fashions is likely to disappear in the near future.

PAPER 4   LISTENING (approximately 40 minutes)

Part 1

You will hear people talking in eight different situations. For questions **1-8**, choose the best answer, **A**, **B**, or **C**.

---

1   In a café, you overhear this man talking to a friend.
    Who is the speaker?

    A   a policeman

    B   a journalist

    C   a shop assistant

> 1

2   You hear part of a radio report about an accident.
    Where did it happen?

    A   on a bridge

    B   on an island

    C   on a road by the sea

> 2

3   You overhear this woman talking to her friend.
    What has she bought?

    A   a jacket

    B   a suit

    C   a shirt

> 3

4   You hear a man talking about his neighbour.
    How did the neighbour respond to the man's complaint?

    A   He was apologetic.

    B   He was embarrassed.

    C   He was unhelpful.

> 4

5 You hear an extract from a radio programme.
What is the man's job?

  A a historian

  B a tour guide

  C a film director

          5

6 On the radio you hear part of a play.
What is the relationship between the speakers?

  A relatives

  B friends

  C colleagues

          6

7 You hear the following on the radio.
What is it?

  A a travel announcement

  B a weather forecast

  C an accident report

          7

8 You switch on the radio and hear a man talking about his scuba
diving experience.
What does he think of it?

  A It was exciting.

  B It was dangerous.

  C It was disappointing.

          8

Part 2

You will hear a talk on an English writer. For questions **9-18**, complete the sentences.

Emily's childhood and background were not very | **9**

Unlike her brothers, she was educated | **10**

With her tutor, she travelled around | **11**

She then produced | **12**

Her relationship with Nathan Fanshaw led to her writing | **13**

She recovered from an illness when a doctor told her to | **14**

Her first novel was called | **15**

The first novel was a | **16**

She gave very good | **17** | from her books.

She did not write her books for | **18**

Part 3

You will hear five people talking about why they like going on holiday without their family or friends. For questions **19-23**, choose which of the statements **A-F** refers to each speaker. Use the letters only once. There is one extra letter which you do not need to use.

Which speaker ...

A   sometimes got fed up with other holidaymakers?

Speaker 1 | **19**

B   enjoyed holidaying alone more than they expected?

Speaker 2 | **20**

C   preferred to stay in the same hotel as before?

Speaker 3 | **21**

D   liked meeting a wide variety of people?

Speaker 4 | **22**

E   liked having something in common with other holidaymakers?

Speaker 5 | **23**

F   found somebody to talk to if they wanted to?

Part 4

You will hear a reporter called Linda Watson talking about her visit to the town of Finstowe. For questions **24-30**, choose the best answer, **A**, **B**, or **C**.

What does Linda say about ...

24   the car parks?

    A   There are not enough of them.
    B   They are too far from the city centre.
    C   They are rather small.

24

25   the shopping area?

    A   It is too busy.
    B   It is easy to find one's way around.
    C   It offers plenty of variety.

25

26   the park?

    A   It is as good as people claim.
    B   It is unsafe for young children.
    C   It has a lot of strict rules.

26

27   the sports facilities?

    A   They are disappointing.
    B   They are expensive.
    C   They are impressive.

27

28   the restaurant?

    A   She liked the food.
    B   She enjoyed the view.
    C   She was pleased with the service.

28

29   the museum?

    A   It is ideal for foreign tourists.
    B   It is most suited to the needs of schoolchildren.
    C   It is particularly interesting to British historians.

29

30   the concert?

    A   It was difficult to get a ticket.
    B   There were lots of tourists there.
    C   It had been poorly advertised.

30

PAPER 5   SPEAKING (14 minutes)

You take the Speaking test with another candidate, referred to here as your partner. There are two examiners. One will speak to you and your partner and the other will be listening. Both examiners will award marks.

Part 1 (3 minutes)

The examiner asks you and your partner questions about yourselves. You may be asked about things like 'your home town', 'your interests', 'your career plans', etc.

Part 2 (4 minutes)

The examiner gives you two photographs and asks you to talk about them for one minute. The examiner then asks your partner a question about your photographs and your partner responds briefly.

Then the examiner gives your partner two different photographs. Your partner talks about these photographs for one minute. This time the examiner asks you a question about your partner's photographs and you respond briefly.

Part 3 (3 minutes)

The examiner asks you and your partner to talk together. You may be asked to solve a problem or try to come to a decision about something. For example, you might be asked to decide the best way to use some rooms in a language school. The examiner gives you a picture to help you but does not join in the conversation.

Part 4 (4 minutes)

The examiner joins in the conversation. You all talk together in a more general way about what has been said in Part 3. The examiner asks you questions but you and your partner are also expected to develop the conversation.

UNIVERSITY *of* CAMBRIDGE
Local Examinations Syndicate

SAMPLE

Candidate Name
If not already printed, write name
in CAPITALS and complete the
Candidate No. grid (in pencil).
Candidate's signature

- -

Examination Title

Centre

Supervisor:

☒ If the candidate is ABSENT or has WITHDRAWN shade here ▭

Centre No.

Candidate No.

Examination Details

0	0	0	0
1	1	1	1
2	2	2	2
3	3	3	3
4	4	4	4
5	5	5	5
6	6	6	6
7	7	7	7
8	8	8	8
9	9	9	9

Candidate Answer Sheet: FCE paper 1 Reading

Use a pencil

Mark ONE letter for each question.

For example, if you think **B** is the right answer to the question, mark your answer sheet like this:

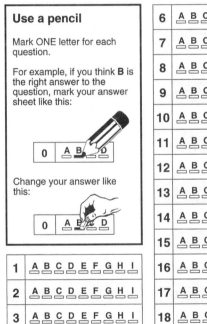

Change your answer like this:

6	A B C D E F G H I
7	A B C D E F G H I
8	A B C D E F G H I
9	A B C D E F G H I
10	A B C D E F G H I
11	A B C D E F G H I
12	A B C D E F G H I
13	A B C D E F G H I
14	A B C D E F G H I
15	A B C D E F G H I
16	A B C D E F G H I
17	A B C D E F G H I
18	A B C D E F G H I
19	A B C D E F G H I
20	A B C D E F G H I

21	A B C D E F G H I
22	A B C D E F G H I
23	A B C D E F G H I
24	A B C D E F G H I
25	A B C D E F G H I
26	A B C D E F G H I
27	A B C D E F G H I
28	A B C D E F G H I
29	A B C D E F G H I
30	A B C D E F G H I
31	A B C D E F G H I
32	A B C D E F G H I
33	A B C D E F G H I
34	A B C D E F G H I
35	A B C D E F G H I

1	A B C D E F G H I
2	A B C D E F G H I
3	A B C D E F G H I
4	A B C D E F G H I
5	A B C D E F G H I

© UCLES K&J Photocopiable

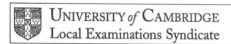

UNIVERSITY *of* CAMBRIDGE
Local Examinations Syndicate

SAMPLE

Candidate Name
If not already printed, write name
in CAPITALS and complete the
Candidate No. grid (in pencil).

Candidate's signature

Examination Title

Centre

Supervisor:

[X] If the candidate is ABSENT or has WITHDRAWN shade here ⊂⊃

Centre No.

Candidate No.

**Examination
Details**

0	0	0	0
1	1	1	1
2	2	2	2
3	3	3	3
4	4	4	4
5	5	5	5
6	6	6	6
7	7	7	7
8	8	8	8
9	9	9	9

Candidate Answer Sheet: FCE paper 3 Use of English

Use a pencil

For **Part 1**: Mark ONE letter for each question.

For example, if you think **C** is the
right answer to the question,
mark your answer sheet like this:

| 0 | A B C D |

For **Parts 2, 3, 4** and **5**: Write your
answers in the spaces next to the
numbers like this:

| 0 | |

Part 1				
1	A	B	C	D
2	A	B	C	D
3	A	B	C	D
4	A	B	C	D
5	A	B	C	D
6	A	B	C	D
7	A	B	C	D
8	A	B	C	D
9	A	B	C	D
10	A	B	C	D
11	A	B	C	D
12	A	B	C	D
13	A	B	C	D
14	A	B	C	D
15	A	B	C	D

Part 2	Do not write here
16	⊂ 16 ⊃
17	⊂ 17 ⊃
18	⊂ 18 ⊃
19	⊂ 19 ⊃
20	⊂ 20 ⊃
21	⊂ 21 ⊃
22	⊂ 22 ⊃
23	⊂ 23 ⊃
24	⊂ 24 ⊃
25	⊂ 25 ⊃
26	⊂ 26 ⊃
27	⊂ 27 ⊃
28	⊂ 28 ⊃
29	⊂ 29 ⊃
30	⊂ 30 ⊃

Turn
over
for
Parts
3 - 5
→

SAMPLE

Part 3		Do not write here
31		31 0 ▭ 1 ▭ 2 ▭
32		32 0 ▭ 1 ▭ 2 ▭
33		33 0 ▭ 1 ▭ 2 ▭
34		34 0 ▭ 1 ▭ 2 ▭
35		35 0 ▭ 1 ▭ 2 ▭
36		36 0 ▭ 1 ▭ 2 ▭
37		37 0 ▭ 1 ▭ 2 ▭
38		38 0 ▭ 1 ▭ 2 ▭
39		39 0 ▭ 1 ▭ 2 ▭
40		40 0 ▭ 1 ▭ 2 ▭

Part 4		Do not write here
41		▭ 41 ▭
42		▭ 42 ▭
43		▭ 43 ▭
44		▭ 44 ▭
45		▭ 45 ▭
46		▭ 46 ▭
47		▭ 47 ▭
48		▭ 48 ▭
49		▭ 49 ▭
50		▭ 50 ▭
51		▭ 51 ▭
52		▭ 52 ▭
53		▭ 53 ▭
54		▭ 54 ▭
55		▭ 55 ▭

Part 5		Do not write here
56		▭ 56 ▭
57		▭ 57 ▭
58		▭ 58 ▭
59		▭ 59 ▭
60		▭ 60 ▭
61		▭ 61 ▭
62		▭ 62 ▭
63		▭ 63 ▭
64		▭ 64 ▭
65		▭ 65 ▭

SAMPLE

Candidate Name
If not already printed, write name
in CAPITALS and complete the
Candidate No. grid (in pencil).

Candidate's signature

Examination Title

Centre

Supervisor:
[X] If the candidate is ABSENT or has WITHDRAWN shade here ▭

Centre No.

Candidate No.

Examination Details

0	0	0	0
1	1	1	1
2	2	2	2
3	3	3	3
4	4	4	4
5	5	5	5
6	6	6	6
7	7	7	7
8	8	8	8
9	9	9	9

Candidate Answer Sheet: FCE paper 4 Listening

Mark test version below

A   B   C   D   E
═   ═   ═   ═   ═

Special arrangements S   H
                      ═   ═

Use a pencil

For **Parts 1** and **3**:
Mark ONE letter for
each question.

For example, if you
think **B** is the right
answer to the
question, mark your
answer sheet like this:

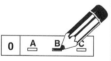

| 0 | A ═ | B ═ | C ═ |

For **Parts 2** and **4**:
Write your answers in
the spaces next to the
numbers like this:

| 0 | EXAMPLE |

Part 1

1	A ═	B ═	C ═
2	A ═	B ═	C ═
3	A ═	B ═	C ═
4	A ═	B ═	C ═
5	A ═	B ═	C ═
6	A ═	B ═	C ═
7	A ═	B ═	C ═
8	A ═	B ═	C ═

Part 2 | | **Do not write here**

9		▭ 9 ▭
10		▭ 10 ▭
11		▭ 11 ▭
12		▭ 12 ▭
13		▭ 13 ▭
14		▭ 14 ▭
15		▭ 15 ▭
16		▭ 16 ▭
17		▭ 17 ▭
18		▭ 18 ▭

Part 3

19	A ═	B ═	C ═	D ═	E ═	F ═
20	A ═	B ═	C ═	D ═	E ═	F ═
21	A ═	B ═	C ═	D ═	E ═	F ═
22	A ═	B ═	C ═	D ═	E ═	F ═
23	A ═	B ═	C ═	D ═	E ═	F ═

Part 4 | | **Do not write here**

24		▭ 24 ▭
25		▭ 25 ▭
26		▭ 26 ▭
27		▭ 27 ▭
28		▭ 28 ▭
29		▭ 29 ▭
30		▭ 30 ▭